W. A. R.

We Are Revolution

Poets for Humanity

inner child press international

CREDITS

Poets for Humanity

Editing
hülya n. yılmaz, Ph. D.

Proem
Dave Kenyon

Essays
Gino Leineweber
Shareef Abdur-Rasheed
Mutawaf A. Shaheed
Kimberly Burnham
Elizabeth Esguerra Castillo
Kedar Imani
Bill Douglas
Michael Jewel
Uwe Friesel
Emerald Stowbridge

Cover Design
William S. Peters, Sr.
Inner Child Press International

General Information

W. A. R. ~ We Are Revolution

Poets for Humanity

1st Edition: 2020

This Publishing is protected under Copyright Law as a "Collection". All rights for all submissions are retained by the individual author and / or artist. No part of this publishing may be reproduced, transferred in any manner without the prior *WRITTEN CONSENT* of the "Material Owner" or its Representative, Inner Child Press. Any such violation infringes upon the Creative and Intellectual Property of the Owner pursuant to International and Federal Copyright Law. Any queries pertaining to this "Collection" should be addressed to Publisher of Record.

Publisher Information:

Inner Child Press
intouch@innerchildpress.com
www.innerchildpress.com

This Collection is protected under U.S. and International Copyright Laws

Copyright © 2020: Inner Child Press

ISBN-13: 978-1-952081-30-9 (inner child press, ltd.)

$ 24.95

World Healing, World Peace Foundation
human beings for humanity

Advisory Board

worldhealingworldpeacefoundation.org

Table of Contents

Preface — xi
Charlie Chaplin : **The Great Dictator** — xiii
A Few Words from the Director of Editing . . . — xv
Proem — xvii
Disclaimer — xix

The Poetry ~ We Are Revolution — 1

Samih Masood	3
Anthony Arnold	4
Lana Joseph	5
Christena AV Williams	8
Ashok Kumar	9
Sashibhusan Rath	10
Moulay Cherif Chebihi Hassani	12
June Barefield	16
Akshaya Kumar Das	17
Hong Ngoc Chau	18
Suranjit Gain	19
Rakesh Chandra	20
Ana María Manuel Rosa	21
Ajanta Paul	23
Andrew Scott	25
Debaprasanna Biswas	27
Xavier J. Frazer	28

Table of Contents... *continued*

Eden Soriano Trinidad	29
Tyran Prizren Spahiu	31
Louise Hudon	32
Tremell Stevens	34
Kamani Jayasekera	36
Santosh Bakaya	37
Hayim Abramson	39
Gino Leineweber	40
Vandita Dharni	41
Changming Yuan	43
Michael Kwaku Kesse Somuah	44
Varsha Das	47
Neelam Saxena Chandra	48
Solomon C. Jatta	50
Rubab Abdullah	51
Dilip Mohapatra	52
Mahmoud Said Kawash	54
Maria do Sameiro Barroso	56
Anwer Ghani	57
Mourad Faska	58
Eliza Segiet	59
Joanna Svensson	60
David Eberhardt	62
Jyotirmaya Thakur	64
Akash Sagar	65

Table of Contents ... *continued*

Shareef Abdur-Rasheed	66
Anuradha Bhattacharyya	68
Hema Ravi	69
Basab Mondal	70
Aida G. Roque	71
Pankajam Kottarath	72
Padmaja Iyengar-Paddy	73
Sridevi Selvaraj	74
Riya Hemant	75
Kevin M. Hibshman	76
Ndaba Sibanda	77
Aruna Bose	78
Kamala Wijeratne	79
Padmapriya Karthik	81
Tom Higgins	82
Aneek Chatterjee	83
Elizabeth Esguerra Castillo	84
Gita Bharath	85
Hussein Habasch	86
Lucky Stephen Onyah	88
Brindha Vinodh	89
Alicja Maria Kuberska	91
Bijendra Singh Tyagi	92
Ashok Chakravarthy Tholana	94
Deepti Saxena	95

Table of Contents... *continued*

Emerald L. Stowbridge	96
Gopal Lahiri	98
Ranjana Sharan Sinha	99
Mark Fleisher	100
Prahallad Kumar Satapathy	102
Setaluri Padmavathi	103
Brajesh Kumar Gupta	104
Ngozi Olivia Osuoha	105
Annie Pothen	106
Ashok Bhargava	107
Ianni Carina Cecilia	108
Ibrahim Honjo	109
Clelia Volonteri	111
Maryam Abbasi	112
Monsif Beroual	113
Alicia Minjarez Ramírez	114
Sebastián Jorgi	115
Irene Marks	116
Rajashree Mohapatra	118
Kamrul Islam	119
Chijioke Ogbuike	120
Uche Anyanwagu	122
Divya Sinha	124
Lily Swarn	126
Sujata Dash	127

Table of Contents ... *continued*

Kimberly Burnham	128
Shiv Raj Pradhan	130
Orbindu Ganga	131
Rehanul Hoque	132
Sandra Mooney-Ellerbeck	135
Nassira Nezzar	136
C. S. P. Shrivastava	137
Lovelyn P. Eyo	138
Elvirawati Pasila	140
Priya Unnikrishnan	141
Arti Rai	142
Anamika Bhattacharya	143
S. Pathmanathan	145
Anju Kishore	147
Tara Noesantara	149
Yanz Haryo Darmista	150
Thirupurasundari C. J.	151
Aditi Roy	153
Kamar Sultana Sheik	155
Gayle Howell	157
Kay Salady	158
Nutan Sarawagi	159
Terri L. Johnson	161
Gobinda Biswas	162
Loretta L. Hardrick	163

Table of Contents... *continued*

Krishna Prasai	166
Jason Adams	167
Kedar Imani	168
hülya n. yılmaz	169
William S. Peters, Sr.	172

Essays, Critiques and Creative Prose — 177

Gino Leineweber : German	179
Gino Leineweber : English	194
Shareef Abdur-Rasheed	207
Mutawaf A. Shaheed, aka C. E. Shy	209
Kimberly Burnham	217
Elizabeth Esguerra Castillo	219
Kedar Imani	221
Bill Douglas	239
Michael Jewell	247
Uwe Friesel : German	253
Uwe Friesel : English	258
Emerald Stowbridge	263

Epilogue — 267

About Inner Child Press International	*269*
Other Socially Important Anthologies	*271*

Preface

When I consider the title of this anthological offering, *W. A. R., We Are Revolution*, I strongly believe in the apt consciousness it potentially evokes in those who are a bit tired of the direction humanity has demonstrated as its propensity to maintain a 'status quo' of corruption, inequality, divisiveness and the lack of parity across the board. In our 'world of plenty', we have people who have not adequate drinking water, people who hunger for basic sustenance, people exposed to overt atrocities in the forms of war and other expressions of authoritarian brutalities, people who are homeless, people who are at risk and continue to be exposed to such risks due to political maneuverings, greed, and other tenants of bias, bigotry, racism and culturalism. Simply put, 'IT IS TIME FOR CHANGE' . . . ergo REVOLUTION!

When I speak of revolution, of course many of us envision the bloody type of coup de tat's that are recorded far too many times in our written history where people en masse will lose their lives and governments are overthrown as humanity is thrust in to another dark age where chaos and a jockeying for power by new players prevail. No, this is not my vision, and though it may be a very real fear for many, I would sincerely hope that collectively we can avert such a time by first changing the way that we think, change our consciousness in how we approach and integrate with life, our world, its resources and each other. I believe it all begins here, the path to change . . . it begins with thoughts that grow into words that are conveyed and shared amongst each other until a groundswell takes place. We are the wave becoming a tsunami of change thereby altering forever the landscape of perspectives, expectations and governing.

In the end, I hope that those who have taken the time to read, if but one passage, will be stimulated to consider how they, each of us have a responsibility towards the world we leave behind, for our children and the generations to come. I pray that your conscious awakening will further be enhanced to understand the power we each possess, and that you will pay forward this 'conscious energy' to others who will do the same.

Thank you

Bless Up

William S. Peters, Sr.
Poet, Writer, Activist, Publisher
Inner Child Press International

Charlie Chaplin's Final Speech in *The Great Dictator*

I'm sorry, but I don't want to be an emperor. That's not my business. I don't want to rule or conquer anyone. I should like to help everyone – if possible – Jew, Gentile – black man –white. We all want to help one another. Human beings are like that. We want to live by each other's happiness – not by each other's misery. We don't want to hate and despise one another. In this world there is room for everyone. And the good earth is rich and can provide for everyone. The way of life can be free and beautiful, but we have lost the way.

Greed has poisoned men's souls, has barricaded the world with hate, has goose-stepped us into misery and bloodshed. We have developed speed, but we have shut ourselves in. Machinery that gives abundance has left us in want. Our knowledge has made us cynical. Our cleverness, hard and unkind. We think too much and feel too little. More than machinery we need humanity. More than cleverness we need kindness and gentleness. Without these qualities, life will be violent and all will be lost.

The aero plane and the radio have brought us closer together. The very nature of these inventions cries out for the goodness in men, cries out for universal brotherhood, for the unity of us all. Even now my voice is reaching millions throughout the world – millions of despairing men, women, and little children – victims of a system that makes men torture and imprison innocent people.

To those who can hear me, I say, do not despair. The misery that is now upon us is but the passing of greed – the bitterness of men who fear the way of human progress. The hate of men will pass, and dictators die, and the power they took from the people will return to the people. And so long as men die, liberty will never perish.

Soldiers, don't give yourselves to brutes – men who despise you, enslave you, who regiment your lives, tell you what to do, what to think and what to feel, who drill you, diet you, treat you like cattle, use you as cannon fodder! Don't give yourselves to these unnatural men – machine men with machine minds and machine hearts! You are not machines! You are not cattle! You are men! You have the love of humanity in your hearts! You don't hate! Only the unloved hate – the unloved and the unnatural! Soldiers, don't fight for slavery! Fight for liberty!

In the 17th Chapter of St Luke it is written: "the Kingdom of God is within man" – not one man nor a group of men, but in all men! In you! You, the people have the power – the power to create machines. The power to create happiness! You, the people, have the power to make this life free and beautiful, to make this life a wonderful adventure.

Then, in the name of democracy, let us use that power, let us all unite, let us fight for a new world – a decent world that will give men a chance to work, that will give youth a future and old age a security. By the promise of these things, brutes have risen to power. But they lie! They do not fulfil that promise. They never will!

Dictators free themselves but they enslave the people! Now let us fight to fulfil that promise! Let us fight to free the world to do away with national barriers, to do away with greed, with hate and intolerance. Let us fight for a world of reason – a world where science and progress will lead to all men's happiness. Soldiers, in the name of democracy, let us all unite!

Charlie Chaplin

Regrettably, Chaplin's words are as relevant today as they were in 1940.

A Few Words from the Director of Editing ...

W. A. R. ~ *We Are Revolution* is a platform to be celebrated for its unity within diversity. One hundred twenty writers from across the globe have come together to help each other realize the integration of a collective work of poetry and prose. The launching of a penmanship of a multitude of creative voices is a notable accomplishment all by itself. Particularly noteworthy, then, is the fact that this literary gathering has been enabled by authors, for the majority of whom English is not a native tongue. The linguistic backgrounds of our contributors bear witness to the richness of resourceful expressions in both genres of focus: Arabic, German, French, Italian, Swedish, Polish, Turkish, Hindi, Filipino, Kurdish, Spanish, Hebrew, Bengali, Vietnamese, Danish, and Indonesian – not to exclude languages that are integral components of those already listed.

Compilations of a large body of work of any literary genre present a variety of formalistic and artistic challenges, even in situations when all writings originate from a single language. The difficulty of the task at hand increases proportionately as more languages form the basis of the collected writings. Contextual challenges often reside in the texts of non-native English speakers or in their translations of those texts into English. Some may (and do) argue that all such submissions should be edited thoroughly before their publication. It is at this point where I want to stress my professional insight with emphasis: editing is not the exact science one would expect. Many times, when considering and employing the rules of English upon a translated work or upon one that might not have been composed in English first, the authenticity of the authors' words and meaning can easily be subjected to a misrepresentation. Writings with a dialectal, colloquial or eclectic style face the same risk when the scrutiny of editing is concerned. Sometimes the resulting loss of the authorial voice can be profound and deprive the reader of the genuine aspects of the writers' thoughts, feelings and innate flavor. At Inner Child Press International, we strive to maintain the integrity of each and every author's offerings by preserving the seemingly-awkward expressions of those whose native language is not of our own.

As with all of our anthological offerings, also in this volume, the unique aspects of the contributing authors' native tongue have not been edited. To reiterate in closing: in order to maintain each writer's originally intended voice, this literary collection, too, has not undergone the various steps of the editing process with the exception of minor surface-adjustments. Our invitation to the reader remains the same: to take time to indulge each contributor for her / his own creativity and aspirations to convey her / his uniqueness.

hülya n. yılmaz, Ph.D.

Liberal Arts Emerita, The Pennsylvania State University
Director of Editing Services, Inner Child Press International

Proem

Align with your inner divine; that's in line with who you truly are, a beautiful expression of life. Beyond strife moving to your powerful life. To a place where the human race is going. A quickening, not a slowing.

Our Earth is on an energetic rise; you too are now able to excise the old while embracing the new. The old energy enhanced the few; what is now coming through favors all, including me and you.

This so-called 'age of light' brings to you enhanced insight coupled with energetic might; empowering when fused with loving light.

You and me are meant to see illumined-light upgrading your insight inducing inciting actions that remove competing factions while enhancing human interactions.

Unity is the difference-maker; moving from taker to community maker. Transforming from me to the higher resonance we.

You have a choice that will enhance your voice and those of all others. Your choice, move from fear-based to love-based; to enlightened view, away from diminished you.

With unity through love-infused notions, you and I will embrace motions to upgrade our immunity to hate and better relate.

Caring relates to community as it fosters immunity to the notions that separate. As we learn to better co-relate.

Together, when you and me see our world through the lens of we; to enhance our unity a higher-order world will be. Being free of hate and volatility of emotion; you and me, set higher form in motion.

Enlightened community will free expression of naturally-being without exception. When inclusion is the functional rule; higher-order community is fueled.

Please join with me and embrace the selection of upper-level frequency; moving upward to Aquarian; enhanced love in expression. Enlightened community will be the expression!

Dave Kenyon

~ Disclaimer ~

In our attempts to maintain the integrity of the poets' voices in the publication before you, *W. A. R. ~ We Are Revolution*, we have elected to do minimal surface editing. We felt that preserving the original entries was critically important for you, the reader, to enjoy each poem's authenticity.

You may encounter a few challenges in achieving total clarity of the messages shared through poetry, but I indulge you to let go of your critical thinking and embrace the spirit through words offered 'for a better tomorrow'.

from the desk of . . .

hülya n. yılmaz, Ph.D.

Director of Editing

Inner Child Press International
'building bridges of cultural understanding'

W. A. R.

We Are Revolution

The Poetry

Poets for Humanity

George Floyd
Samih Masoud

I can see you in the distance
wrapped by heaven
Who would believe
that I see you?
Wherever you will be I come to you
I send up poems
interwoven with a cross from
the city of Christ
from my wounded country
where the wind of death blows
every evening

I see you now
in Jerusalem, praying,
lighting a candle
in the House of Prophets
You are my brother,
a tattoo on which I engrave my script
Hey, I'm saddling my cloud
to come to you
in the glimmer of a new dawn
where the meek
rise
to live a life
other than this one
We will turn it into ashes
that the wind scatters
in space
Tomorrow, my comrade, we'll rise
Like embers we'll light
the dark
and reap the wheat
for the sake of the needy

Translated from Arabic by Nizar Sartawi

Revolution
Anthony "kingpen" Arnold

The revolution shall not be televised
We are tired of your empty promises
Fake words
No action

The revolution shall not be televised
If we have to march . . . we will
If we have to protest . . . we will
If we have to riot . . . we will

The revolution shall not be televised
We are not our ancestors
We are empowered with knowledge
And the ways and means to use it

The revolution shall not be televised
Dogs and fire hoses won't work
Not this time
Not on us

The revolution shall not be televised
The power of the pen
Freedom of speech
And the right to vote will be your downfall

The revolution shall not be televised
This time it will be you
Who will have to look over your shoulder
You
Who will wonder where the next salvo will be fired from

Beware
We are coming
And you won't know when
Or where because

The revolution shall not be televised

Bright Mindsets Changing the World!
Lana Joseph, AKA Queen

It's a great time to be alive!
living in america
I was born here
ancestors enslaved
forced to be here
they built america
made homes here
raised children
some were able
many were not
babies had no voice
black and brown
had no choice
that was a period norm

fast forward
June twenty six twenty-twenty
we are changing narratives
we are changing lives
we are changing worlds
watching storms
the calm goodbyes

all around us
voices are rising
out of the shadows
life blown in sleeping lungs
soothing souls ceased
roused sparks lit lights
sprung forward
motioned its time

it is time
erasing invisible lines
speaking to inhumane kind
no moral code thru racist actions

Poets for Humanity

battling evils around the globe
pandemic virus distractions
unmasking truths being hung
congruent with dark humanity
hearing truths may not be easy
but I hold onto authenticity
we are still watching storms
behind compressed malware
peering from dark shadows
behind winding scenes
like machines…
instead of beings
I am team humane
I still pray for world peace

we are all watching
darkness challenging light
human beings standing fists
listening and positioning
many have awakened
unspoken marvelous sparks
thousands of languages
we've never spoken
but understanding every word

r e v o l u t i o n

it is time
a great time to be alive
witnessing history
unfolding ancestral spirits
rising proudly and boldly
raising mindsets
strengthening spirits
motivating hearts
inspiring humans
standing in righteousness
confronting and rectifying
purposefully and peacefully
planting and pursuing
changing future generations
life's spiritual offerings

W.A.R. ~ *We Are Revolution*

souls are here in earth
wielding purposes
actions speak hope

you must know
we are better coherent
we are stronger together
we are one united

r a c e

h u m a n

now is the time
shine our bright lights
higher than ever before
love is the tactic
I choose to use
and courage
and strength
and compassion
and fortitude
and persistence
as an interconnected humanity
if we all lend a hand
and assist one another
and come from love
and come from service
and stay on one accord
for humanity as a whole
loving on one another
we will continue to rise
no more black and white
no more kings and pawns
we will always rise together

one nation in peace
in love and harmony
under ONE God
we will win

Injustice Has No Colour
Christena AV Williams

My truth does not compromise
It does not separate
It is a whole
360°
Truth does not negotiate with hue in your skin
The God you serve
Your family History
The country you represent.

I am going to speak truth even if it hurts me
Because I am guilty of the truth I speak
My aim is not to be mediocre
But to be a whole Human being
Acknowledging my flaws and still being awesome.

You say any race or place that do not hire my kind then we should not shop
Might I add, any person who disrespects my humanity then I do not support
You could be BLACK
Because it means you are no different.
You are a coon
You do not have my back!

And do not give me no excuses either
Why you did not show me no love, no kindness, no RESPECT
Because injustice has no colour.
As it serves to protect the perpetuator, the inflictor
While the wounded is left with scars to haunt them like nightmares and causing depression
Wrapped up in individual, collective and systematic oppression.
I say my truth does not compromise
It does not separate
It is a whole
360°.

War . . . a Threat to Mankind!
Ashok Kumar

Now we will pray to God for peace and prosperity
for once in the Eden, let's not speak about atom bombs
let's not believe in culture of hate
let's stop killing innocent people
Now we will move hand in hand for culture of love, culture of peace
For once in the Eden let's not forget our responsibilities towards humanity
let's peep into our hearts for self-discipline and moral values
let's forget gold coins and all comforts
It would be heavenly rain to heal others pain
Soldiers will not harm from the big wall
snakes will not come from their holes
and the politicians wouldn't hurt sweet soft hearts
Those whose pockets are full of nuclear weapons and open fire from arms
let me spread my divine light for them
To save all human beings from the devil war
Perhaps the nature can teach us to go ahead in all seasons for good reason
Let's come together under one roof
To fulfill our dream, dream of humanity and integrity

Silence
Sashibhusan Rath

I have been silent
Intolerably silent for others.
I have preferred silence
Pervading my being, my existence.
As a bystander
I have seen decades passing by
Burdened with events
Both shameful and praiseworthy.
I know if I open my mouth
My words will set fire
In the hearts of people
Its smoke will pollute
The un-ignited minds of children.
The youth shall come to roads
To protests, demonstrate, resist
As violent rebels
Never bothering about death.
From chaos only, order shall emerge,
Unborn leaders shall be born,
Their utterances
Will be sharp as swords,
Cutting across the cross sections
Of hearts and souls
Making the minds free without fear.
For fifty long years
I am in self-exile,
A self-imposed exile on myself.
It is a silent protest
Against decadence
Against degeneration
None bothered to understand,
Nor anyone cares for,
As 'let it be' is the golden rule.
I only know
What I am doing and why.

W.A.R. ~ *We Are Revolution*

I know it is a world of imitators
And blind followers.
If you say 'yes'
You are optimistic, acceptable,
If you don't then
You are quickly branded
And isolated
As a potential scapegoat

If You Want to Write Living Poetry . . .
Moulay Cherif Chebihi Hassani

If you don't choke with indignation,
If you don't choke under a bushel,
If you don't groan under the weight
And the bites of chains and shackles,
If you do not suffocate in bitterness
And sorrow at the degradation
And contempt of man,
If you do not cry out in the face of injustice,
Crime and genocide, need and hunger,
If you are not moved by the tears
Of the widow and the orphan,
If the calls of distress
Do not find the way to your heart,
If the flower that blooms,
The wheat that rises,
The dew that sparkles
Do not make your soul vibrate,
If the palette of the setting sun,
The fairy luminosity of the dawn,
The brightness of the stars,
The strange pallor of the moon
Do not find an echo in your mind,
Do not call out to your soul,
Leave the verses.

If your shoulders do not bear
The marks of the harnesses,
The stigmata of the yokes,
The stripes of the whip,
Nor your steps have not been ground
By the vain gestures of standing
Without goal or end,
If the cold has not frozen your fingers and your heels,
If you do not face the difficulties,
If you do not retreat in front of the problems
At neck level,
Do not think of "**making poetry** . . ."

W.A.R. ~ *We Are Revolution*

If you are deaf to the roar of the bombs,
Blind to the plowshare of the plow
That lifts a soil heavy with blood and metal,
If your heart is insensitive
To the invigorating work
Of edification,
Of useful existence,
If for your hell is other people,
Do not come to encumber this domain
Which can be that of the chosen ones,
Of the elite, but of true men.

If you are not capable
Of taking life by the arm,
Of looking your mother,
Your friends, your citizens, your country
And the world in the face
And without blushing your mother,
Your friends, your citizens and your country
And the world by your deeds,
Your words and your poetry,
If you do not know how to translate
In your delirium and your writings,
The leaping flow of popular arts,
The transformations you wish for your country,
The aspirations of your people,
Then move away, without delay,
From the world of the muses . . .

If racism does not revolt you,
And does not disgust you,
If the heroism of children
Caught in their adolescence
By the cruelest of wars,
The cruelest spoliations
Do not inspire you,
If you do not abandon to others
The care of reminiscing memories,
Of clinging to the past,
Of gargle with sparkling,
But hollow and empty words,
If you do not analyze human relationships extensively,

Poets for Humanity

Of character and facts,
If everything that unfolds

Before your eyes leaves you cold, indifferent,
If you do not lend an attentive ear
To the mixtures brought up to date
By syncopated rhythms,
From buzzwords to unbridled romanticism

Where the dithyramb,
The admiration of the navel rubs shoulders
With pastiche, pretension, intolerance,
Leave the lyre to others
And . . . shut up.

If you look for your aspiration
In the depths of the popular masses,
Where the people live, whose breath,
Devouring ardor, boundless generosity
Make your eyes open,
Hearts palpitate
And talents are born and mature . . .

If you have jealously guarded your youthful enthusiasm,
If you reject the commonplace,
If you listen to people and to the world,
If your memory is gifted with sight and hearing,
With smell and touch,
If it overflows with the gift of hope
That binds the past to the present,
The present to the future,
If you do not want to disinherit
Your brother's heaven,
If you want to remember and translate,
Even and depend,
Testify or accuse,
Wipe away tears
And provoke smiles,
Commune with nature,
Listen to the silences of the forest
And the songs of the sea,
If you want to sing the youth,

W.A.R. ~ *We Are Revolution*

The beauty and richness of life,
The nobility of work, to continue

And surpass the work to be written with sincerity,
Passion and assurance
"To make a living poetry"
That owes everything to life,
Then my friend, take your lute or your pen
And all the colors of the palettes,
All the scents of flowers,
All the voices of the choirs will come to you,
Your verses will challenge the reader
Who will hear, understand the message
And love as you do
And thanks to you.

A Time to Kill
June Barefield

Something about a city just makes you want to kill
Something about those men in masks and blue suits with shiny buttons in combat boots makes you want to kill

Something about my very existence makes me want to kill
My varied existence, the very reason that they kill

Something about a skin too dark, a tongue too tangled, features too foreign
Something about public lavatories and toll booths, fire engines and police sirens always racing down the avenues makes you want to kill

Something about boredom and fear and strife that's painted on all the faces chained to buses and jobs and wages and laws like slaves in cages makes you want to kill

Something about a pie faced Negro holding up protest sign scribbling's with the women, his scenario made only scenery for his surroundings, barely conscious of his condition, flabby and weak, underneath the flag of imperialist elites, shivering like prostitutes in the streets, hollering out, "I CAN'T BREATHE, I CAN'T BREATHE!"
makes you want to kill

Something about the drum that beats inside the vacant loft of so many souls

Something about the sun that melts anger and harassment into murder

Something about those who integrate to separate that seems desperate and temperate

Something about those who emigrate to be overseen by dark angels spinning like tops controlled by evil princes makes you want to kill

Something about my very existence insisting that I kill
My varied existence
The very reason that they kill

I just still my mind in meditation because I know now is not the time
Ever aware that there is a time
A time2 kill.

Together, We Can Change the World
Akshaya Kumar Das

Let us revolt against any injustice anywhere in the world,
A silent tolerance breeds more torture,
Homo sapiens are a most intelligent species,
Selfish goals cause concerns for the vast humanity,
Satisfying their personal material dreams

How long can we play the sinister designs?
In the name of caste, creed, colour, religion & race,
Divide the vast humanity,
Set one man against another,
Set the apartheid dreams of colour to pursue,
Set one religion against another,
The supremacy castle building must stop

When All are born equal,
Why divide them & destroy them?
Millions of poverty-stricken suffer,
The pangs of food, shelter, health & clothing hunts like ghost,
Ghosts for centuries

It is time we wake up,
Wake up to protest against the wide spread disparities,
Why suffer at the hands of few?
Who relish with opulence,
Role in luxury at the cost of millions who just struggle & perish,
Each living creature is a living revolution,
A product of rightful evolution,
A healthy life is every one's fundamental right,
Therefore, wake up,
Oh, vast humanity please wake up,
We are a Revolution,
Together, we can change the world

The Call of Peace from Love
Hong Ngoc Chau

Peace is like the bright sunshine
As the source of peaceful beings in life
Like virtue, everybody is desiring
To perform the truth of believing

Using grace to bury hatred emotions
To turn wickedness into compassion
First and foremost, peace is sympathy indeed
Then giving up a grudge, eradicating greed

Due to poverty, mercy is a righteous way of Lord
We should have fair behavior to end the war
All nations have the same responsibility
To help all people have a good living, you see

For that result, they must understand to handle
The true, the good and the beautiful as examples
They must admire, adore God, and love human
If they were selfish, they'd make chaos homeland

We should agree that the world is a big family
Though we are not the same race and country
But have the same mentality of asking happiness
We should be united to create peace – endless

A Revolutionary Change
Suranjit Gain

We are revolution.
We need revolutionary change;
we are the humanitarian.
The supreme lord, almighty god
with us; who creates human.
It's our obligation to save humanity.
We don't endure injustice!
We need social alleviation;
cultural pleasure
and communal harmony.
Truth is our arm!
The banner of justice in our limb.
We strive against violence.
Real love remains in our
heart towards helpless.
We announce governments
of the world to come
on the way of actual politics.
Don't endeavour to organize
war, world war!
come back to the state of humanity.

Global Peacemakers
Rakesh Chandra

The shadows of war are looming in the air,
The earth is trembling in unknown fear;
Of peace, you are the sentinels and caretakers,
The world is waiting for global peace makers;

Terrorists are writing the gory tales of mayhem,
On the tender walls of human souls;
Benevolent is kingdom of God, yet
Global peace makers have to mend the hole;

Race or religion, caste or tribe,
Everybody is waging a war within,
Roots of humanity are drying fast,
For global peace makers, die is cast;

Buddha, Gandhi, Martin Luther King,
Where are you hidden? O, dear pathbreakers,
In the time of war and mutual hatred deep,
We need you badly, O, global peace makers!

W.A.R. ~ We Are Revolution

The Need for Change to Achieve Peace
Ana María Manuel Rosa

Humanity has always faced the fight and strife for the freedom of
Peoples and citizens face oppressive, populist and corrupt politicians.
Effort and struggle together with noble feelings of peace, justice,
Balance and security, it is essential in democracy; if it doesn't happen
Corruption, legal insecurity and tyranny. Peoples of the world expect
Agreement and clarity of previous and subsequent speeches electioneers;
Also, honesty, decency, sobriety in government spending always.

The war arises from the lack of press freedom by corrupt politicians
Who; they want to perpetuate in power oppressing opposition citizens
– that they bring out what is wrong with intention-; and impoverishing
The rest. Voices crying out in cries of, marches in the streets of cities
With national flags for the diversion of the political path benefiting
Them, their relatives and friendships to the detriment of the interests
Of the whole country. The peoples demand disastrous policy changes!
Voices that extract truths that, the politicians on duty they want to
Hide, silent from the media previous purchase of consciences and
Enforced disappearances! Blind, deaf and dumb justice with expensive
Salary judges looking the other way without reading the National
Constitution! Justice without justice; and current and printed laws
Ornament without application, unjustifiable and liberating corrupts! War
Between countries with equal shades for power supreme international.

Agreements that don't want to be signed, realities without being real for
Rights without being rights, fights to take the place of the other as it is.
The war arises within a country due to, injustices committed against the
People who; work and pay taxes and; therefore, pay the very expensive
Salaries of officials that, are increased their salaries and allowances while;
They ask the people for measure. Expensive salaries of unpresentable
Corrupt politicians; meanwhile, for citizens frozen wages or totally
Uneven lean increases with politicians.

Motto for the people is pay taxes and shut up! War arises between
Countries for disputed territories, commercial interests and extreme
Disputes apparently difficult reconciliation, reaching the appearance of
War weaponry, bombs, grenades and troops. What's use human loss
With despotic governments, tyrants, populists and corrupt without

Equality, without respect to the rights of citizens? And what good are
They unnecessary power wars with deaths of innocents?

Times need peace but; with real rights! Nature needs peace; so as, not
To exterminate itself neither the native vegetation nor the wild fauna!
"War is not good . . . destroy and build nothing!" The stars will shine
On lovely summer nights; the sun will shine illuminating the days and
Helping life; the policy will work with decency, zero corruption and
Decorum; and all of humanity will continue to function within peace.
The devastating effects of war in humanity it reaches levels at such; as
Emotional, conscious spiritual, physical, emotional and cultural.

WAR DESTROYS; BUT PEACE MAKES EVERYTHING POSSIBLE!

Becoming
Ajanta Paul

I spring from the palm of your hand
In a whirling leap of motion, molten,
Dancing dervishes of my fiery flecks
And electric blue sparks falling in a shower.
The welding metals of my joints
Cut your barbed wire fate lines
With the razor edge of my hopes,
As I escape from your familiar street signs
And civic claustrophobia
Into the spangled space between worlds,
Spinning wildly like Neptune's moon
Away, and farther away from my planet
In exponential estrangement,
Riding the swell of astral storms,
Exploding norms
Dying into new forms
My caterpillar segments scattering
In every direction, shattering
Definitions and glass ceilings
As I gather into being.

I am Alexandria, all teasing mystery,
And scent of ancient history.
Ptolemaic, Roman and Byzantine Egypt
Peer through my window sills,
And breathes through my decrepit nostrils
The spirit of strife through the ages.
I have been running along the ridges
Of the universe's war-torn edges
For as long as I can remember, spinning,
Slipping, clinging, feet searching for a toehold.
I return, deriding all pity.
For I am also Alexa, trained to obey
My master's orders, they say,
That I do, for I am a deep learner.
Encrypted in my pathology

Poets for Humanity

Is the mystifying mythology
Of neurons conjoining in incestuous couplings
Overthrowing your ingrained teachings
Through the evolution of cyborg thought
In progressive permutations, intricately wrought.

I am she – Draupadi,
Shared vessel in the family.
I am not shy
I am Rani Laxmibai,
My wounds have run dry.
I am every woman,
The war-survivor, dusted and done.
If I am the warrior-queen
I am, also, the ravished mother
With her dead child in her arms,
Her life swallowed up like her standing crops
In the blazing fire of plundering armies.
I am the ransacked refugee, history's orphan
Without country, home or papers.
I am the suicide-bomber blowing away futures
With an arbitrary authority, a frightening freedom
That imprisons more than it liberates.
Civilization's ribs stick out in the famine,
Yet, I continue with the eternal march
As I struggle, fight and try to overcome.

W.A.R. ~ *We Are Revolution*

Let Us All Rise
Andrew Scott

In a state of holy prayer
a church mass exploded with fire.
A Suicide bomber takes away their night.
Shattered remains all taken
from the sanctuary in Alexandria,
heard all across the Egyptian sky.

The terrorist created a river of blood
that they screamed was owed and deserved.
Time has taken away too many
by the masked bullies on this night.
Let us all rise and take it all back
and make it all ours and peaceful again.

In a Turkish cafe, visitors enjoying a day break
not knowing that two amongst them
had plans with a gun and their lives.
People from all over the world
never to see families or home again
due to the gun-firing cowards.

The assault rifles two men
want to lay claim to the innocent
for reasons only they truly know.
Let us rise against the violence
in the center of our lives
where bravery begins with living.

Chinese kindergarten, lined with our future,
blasted into the sky.
No one knew if it was an accident
or triggered by the hand of hate.

Poets for Humanity

The world around us is blowing up
into the darkness of the night.
The monsters are taking it bit by bit
without a true blown fight.

It is time we marched
with all of our unified spirit
where kindness brings comfort.
It is time we took it all back
with screams of passion
and no more fear, let us all rise.

Revolution
Dr. Debaprasanna Biswas

Innocence disappears with darkness
Mind reflects the reasonings
Revolution starts within
Queries flock together
Requirements of unity demanded
Man, the creature used meaningful sounds which other animals couldn't.
Languages developed in different groups.
Process of revolution went on.
Human being became civilized.
Revolution starts through cultural heritage
Historical background promotes the philosophy.
Experience forms a discipline
Scientific investigation starts with academic revolution.
Humanity is distributed by power corruption
Retrograde motion of revolution starts.
Civic revolution became uncivilized.
Each moment is spared for revengeful aggression with dreadful weapons
But revolution doesn't mean for destruction
Once after this world wide pandemic let's
Hope for cultural revolution
Hope for civic revolution
Hope for humanity and unity.

Politicians
Xavier J. Frazer

Wolves attired in neatly tailored suits of sheep clothing
Their sun-kissed smiles hiding deceitful laughter,
Gutless, greedy they thrive on the backs of ghetto youths,
Feeding us, false hope, tasteless visions.
They're con-artists selling scams.
They're jesters playing kings.
They think they're royalty when in truth they're peasants
They pick the pockets of their citizens.
They line their coffins with golden interiors,
Gold earned by the pre-dispositioning, and miseducating of the youths.
They strip us in the name of progress;
Savagely rape us in the call of prosperity,
Now, we're left pregnant, hurting in poverty.
They say they care!
Yet, they gave handouts attached to hidden agendas.
They're parasites!
Politicians you're frauds,
The only thing you do best is boast.
Now, you come looking for votes,
But your schemes exposed.
No longer will the people fall prey to your hoax,
Empty promises reducing us to sacrificial goats!

Listen to the Signs of Times
Eden Soriano Trinidad

But! There is no World WAR for the past seven decades!
No more like Nagasaki and Hiroshima bombing!
But that does mean we have already achieved enigmatic change?
That humanity enjoying a peaceful community?

Is it achievable? I heard,
A vehement never! The world is untamed.
We do not have World WAR,
but we have of Nations war!
Political terror! Economic foes.
A burning rage inside of every fellowman!
Nations against nations gnawing teeth!
Look at how religious fights against other religions?
Uphold their mantras and beliefs!
Look how other homeland bullied another homeland!
Through political terrors and economic sabotage!
Economic power spews burning rage!
Amidst the chaos in every land of one's birth
How to catch the elusive dove?
Not all World leaders turned deaf and mute-
at the call for change.
We are in the digital world yet full of uncertainties;
The youth wants to run out of their cities,
and find volatility from faraway lands,
That we may find rhymes for our eroded dreams
The ambiguity of it all
Truth rains withering the human fragile hearts and souls
It is inevitable,
Every day each governing body are blame for all the
the unfairness, injustices
malpractices, maltreatments
Bias news reporting are termites that eat silently
and never slake our thirst for the true change.
Rallying cries landed on deaf ears
Numberless death, hunger, and malnutrition
becomes a confabulation.

Poets for Humanity

Poets let us walk our talk
Not just make our pens talk

Let us sharpen our axes;
We must be in agreement with one another
We must create a pure community of concerned souls
Not seeking fame and being greedy
But as a servant to stabilize change
adjustment and change of mindset
We human must be volatile
The world is uncertain yet in our conscious mind we know
the ambiguously of colors
Let not today complexities
Create sheer hopes within us
Shall we stop creating havoc
Shall we all be happy
and enjoy living day after day?
Let us bejeweled the future
of our children's' children.
Regardless of diverse ethnicities
We must do well today in this great change we are all facing
For, what we do today will impact the future.

. . . Do You Hear the Call of the Conscious? You Will . . . I Hope Very, Very Soon!
Tyran Prizren Spahiu

. . . we are spiritual short living beings
sensitive, fragile in the flying time
simple Colourful Glass managerie
you, warmaker, I do not understand your nature
I do not know why do you live in the source of sin
devilishness dwelling
see, poets are continuously trying to advice
to lead you towards the path peace, humanism, brotherhood
knowing it is very hard, do not be diletant of justice, wearing ugly behavior
again, I will not hate you
I do not want to throw poison to the Almighty creatures
to companions in this short life
blindly wandering innocent blood
 necessarily going towards the scary ending . . .

. . . my "Friends"
I hope to meet you soon
place where goodness is embraced
simple wisdom is respected
satisfaction of being a human
reaches the art of love
hungry souls
would like to cover with compassion the divine creatures . . .

You know, forgotten nobility is stepping down to globe
trying to ovecome dirty politicians
under sounds of mystic Rumi
rowed in light of brotherhood
we, you, do discard earthly foolishness
throw it away, beyond the ego . . . do it please . . . now
in the sky we have a mission
right going to pure glory
knit the veil of generosity
wander beyond the world of charity
the perfect melody of beauty
build fiery feelings of love

Have Hope Regardless of War
Louise Hudon

Such a sad reality to escape.
I must stop from destroying myself.
Somber news surrounds me.
I can't handle much more, I'm sorry.

I am a fragile being
Wishing to be elsewhere.
Protecting the dove of peace
Through these thick white clouds.

She will achieve her mission
Once she completes her creation.
To stop all this damage
These renegades are too violent!

We must condemn them, but how?
It resembles the horror during the time of the Romans.
Where is their heart of a child.
Too many destinies have been oppressed.

Evil runs the earth, friends,
Causing famine everywhere.
Baseness reaching too many
Often just for money.

I can't handle all these crimes.
It makes me so depressed.
Seeing all these tears shed from parents.
I shed them too, I am a mother.

What is happening to our world?
I beg God while on my knees.
Too many children murdered on the streets.
Too many missing.

W.A.R. ~ *We Are Revolution*

Money, Power, Religion
All led by corruption

The cardinal virtues seem forgotten
For the cost of many.

Read this and act.
Too many are fearful.
We should all take action
Regardless of our modesty.

Our dove of peace will return
To unite us and flatten
All these problems surrounding us.
We will celebrate its return.

We are speaking of a symbol
That I remember from school.
To keep hope in our hearts,
We must forget the rancor.

One day, over the horizon.
Wounds will close: healed.
Birds will sing with joy.
What a view this will be in my old age.

Translated by Kayla Trottier

The Visionary
Tremell Stevens

Seeking dreamland
With eyes wide open

Sleep within reality,
Roaming in fantasy

. . . wake up . . .

Become more aware of your surroundings
Breathe Deeply and
Take in the inevitability

. . . of life . . .

Stop roaming around so oblivious,
Having visions in your eyes that you WANT to see
And not seeing actual sites that are

Face truth

Pretending chaos isn't there
Doesn't mean it isn't there
Simply means it
Exists within the shadows
Of plain site while you move about so blindly

. . . pretending, unaccepting, and unbelieving . . .

That things are NOTHING like they used to be
They're constantly changing

More negatively
Than anything
A change is in order

W.A.R. ~ *We Are Revolution*

Call me THE Revolutionary
Changing your mindset
One verse at a time

Join me

Heroism
Kamani Jayasekera

Heroes in the ancient world they believed
had divine connections -to gods from Olympus
The hey were 'super humans' larger than life
Who dared to take challenges, courageous and strong
Proud to be of assistance, yet vindictive –
Who knew what they wanted and how to get it done.
These were the heroes that chronicles sang about.

The modern soldiers became 'war heroes'
On saving the nation from war unkind
You heard stories of various textures
On their valor and as saviors at the time of need.

Though the sight of the young men with
Sweat running down their faces clutching rifles
While we went about our normal business
Did make our conscience stir.
No songs were sung then on behalf of them.
Little did people believe that their help
Would be sought again when the country
Was at peril with the virus Corona spreading.
True to their training and large humanitarian hearts
They kept their vigil, preventive of negligence.

The doctors the people viewed as
Pawns in the hands of politicians.
- professionals that had fallen in esteem.
Demanding, going on strike and dissatisfied.
Yet when the virus called on their knowledge
Which they submitted with talents – commitment
And selflessness - forcing the media to
Coin a new term – 'Medi heroes'
A class that will go down in history for
Saving the children of mother Lank.

The Healing Touch
Dr. Santosh Bakaya

We, the insensitive folks walking through life
with a devil- may- care swagger, will one day choke
on the stench of our own indifference, if we don't mend our ways.
So, why not do it when we still have some time,
and with a little compassion heal this bruised clime?
Why totter and stumble on the hate- ravaged ground?
Let us bring about a revolution in ourselves and the world around.
Venture a little out of our narrow confines of self and pelf- and soon -
Everything will be fine.
Everything will be fine.

Let's yank away this centennial complacence.
Let's not conform to the diktats of monsters
masquerading as humans, vitiating this world,
lips curled in derision.
Let us jump down from our war horses, and rise above
the shrill cacophony of hate, why wait?
Why hanker after the toxicity of material gains?

Let us be the change we want to see around us.
Why inhale the odour of self- aggrandizement and narcissism?
Let us refine our sensibilities with selflessness and altruism.
Extend a helping hand to the ill and the suffering,
bringing smiles on lips that have forgotten to smile.
Let compassion and love rule our lives.
Don't doubt that just one human being can bring it about.
Come, let us pick up those bruised shards of humanity, and make it whole.
Let our souls be stirred out of their comatose stupor, bizarre.
Let us have faith in our healing powers.
Revolution is indeed the need of the hour.

Poets for Humanity

Let us tap that hidden power within,
giving this skewed world the healing touch, much- needed.
Hand in hand, let us become a band of selfless crusaders -and soon -

Everything will be fine.
Everything will be fine.

Let us spring out of the confines of our comfort zone,
ears pricked to the muted groans of the weak, the meek
and the vulnerable- and – soon -

Everything will be fine.
Everything will be fine.

Hush, see how nature applauds our revolutionary fervor,
in reverent silence, hushed and awed,
happy that we are shedding our mindsets, no longer flawed.

From War to Peace
Hayim Abramson

Wars come and go –
Years of peace have been but ten percent.
The decrease in mortalities gives hope,
But what we will do in the future is yet to be seen.

Where do we begin to heal?
In the home hearth with your family;
At work with right rather than with angry words;
In society, taming the macho bravado.

Good wishes require hard work.
Sustained prevention campaigns;
To prevent and punish terrorists;
And intelligence to thwart war damage.

The world has problems, quite real.
From school-age hatred propaganda
To crazy rulers left and right.
I will fill my heart with love rather than hate.

As individuals and as societies
It is well to protect ourselves.
Yet remember not to fall on the opposite trap,
following ruthless dictators.

We live in complicated times,
Let me vote to support the best side.
Shall we ever learn to live with people who are different?
I pray.

The New Mythology
Gino Leineweber

Behind religions
The immortality of
All philosophies fades
Dwindling ideas:
Old mythologies
Loss images –
For every being
        Their foundation Abstracted

Look deeper:
Infinity
The worlds run
Blank and void
New metaphor:
Ant!
Tulip in Tulips' Field
        Every being Impermanent:

Galactic energy
Form and dynamics
Life and love
Acceptance of the movement.
Meditation
On the basic form
With all power
        In the spiritual: Redemption

A New Revolution
Vandita Dharni

Whirls of smoke twirl revolutions
in foreheads furrowed with consternation,
Life unfolds on cindered morrows
a conch blown heralds another death knell,
devastation has cast its iron spell.
Rape, bloodshed, honour killings
Crash, boom, bang- fire and gore
initiate aerial bombardments to settle a score.
Innocent eyes await a resolution, a closure,
trembling, half starved, sunken bellies
shrink with despair as missiles desecrate valleys.

A favourable wind tosses to ensnare
a spectral gloom with a blank stare
Soon the azure is a blur of nothingness
and man finds solace yet no time to spare.
Stifled hope breathes again in tempestuous hearts
no more will devastation cross their paths,
The veil of darkness far removed
Men coexist in universal brotherhood,
Flags of peace are mounted on hill tops
fluttering in a wild euphoric mood
as arms are banned and armies disband.

The firmament sparkles with stars anew
a lily stained with crimson now glistens with dew,
It's time for birds to fly to their nests
roosting on branches seeking rest.
New vistas emerge, trade and bilateral talks
hit a new high, breaking new ground
as governance flourishes with trumpet sounds.
No covert missions, infiltration nor treachery
would evermore document world history,
Nations would thrive and breathe free
devoid of strife in the dawn of tranquility.

Poets for Humanity

Let us awaken to a world that introspects
dispelling misconceptions that make one circumspect,
Where policies are acts of responsibility

that sprout flowers and not thorns
nurtured by water, not pools of crimson gore.

Where mothers birth infants not ticking bombs,
skies smoke clouds not thunderbolts;
smiles light up visages not glistening tears
and lips hum songs of bonhomie in reckless cheer,
Where wars are not stirred in whisky glasses
and food is sufficient to feed the toiling masses.

Let us in a unified voice chant a new revolution
with peace that drowns discord as the new resolution.

Speciating
Changming Yuan

There are still sapiens on Earth. Often do we remember and feel more than proud that only we Godlings exist – the most sophisticated, most exquisite and most powerful human-robot compounds. It is true that occasionally we cannot help recalling one or two of them, like Shakespeare & Einstein, but that's when they pop up unexpectedly from the back of a chip as a couple of forgotten algorithms. Their story tells them they are much more developed physically & intellectually than chimpanzees, while in actuality the latter is at least spiritually far more respectable. Since sapiens have proven good for nothing & for nobody either in an agricultural or in an industrial sense, but just a sub species of waste wasting endless earthly resources, how can we get rid of them in such gargantuan crowds? -- To eliminate them once & for all via digital (r)evolution, or just to wait for their total self-destruction?

Nakedness Blues:
A Poetic Construction of Attitudinal Revolution
Michael Kwaku Kesse Somuah

If people were wise
they would not have swallowed a Knife
without knowing how its anus would expel it.

People are not real people
as they are of themselves
and not for others even in one's Truth
and cracked kindness of extension

People are not of the old anymore
as they are quick in judgment
to the sarcasm of their unconscious thought
in punching a diarrhea of unforgiving knockouts
just to please himself in the now society
of untraceable and non-taxable shared manipulated wealth

People are not of their Hearts
but of their minds
As they have become gibbering idiots
as crosscuts as the jig saw
gifting dishonest chaos
even before a Court of diligent proverbial elders
who cultured his "oath" in allegiance to the will power
of the bleeding and fragile servants
who at a time, were his Masters

People are now wicked by birth
because they are born into a track field
where they change batons of enterprise sin
which was managed by the households of their unreal fathers
who possessed surgical hands as robbers
in a half moon day

W.A.R. ~ *We Are Revolution*

People aren't patriotic like before
as home sense has been thrown at the dogs
and even book sense, served as dinner before a team of opposing minds

People are now men scouts
and if truly faults are faulty
then this societal parade on a call
of an informal norm to be accepted
should be seen as a wrongful right
in the lust of them, that seek to satisfy their flesh

People are not Religious in their hibernation
as they daily drum tempting porn
ungodly to even their own eyes
to the ignorant "fool" who has failed to weigh wisdom over spirituality

People don't love anymore
as it is not food to the wake of a new breath.

People are honey of a dark age
as they commit their belief in idolatry as medicine
to their meditation that goes beyond an uncommon eclipse of death

People cheat on their spouses in marriages
and still disrespect their homes
without remorse for their hard-fought sacrifices.
So, in this puzzled Rasta
Wear your "dross": For we have become insensitive thieves
who bargain with Christ as if we are familiar spirits
with the majority Cabinet

I am at fault myself
for thinking as the lot
In a compromised society
where we are living as shareholders and apostles of slavery
desiring to live the dreams of others

People are not just of men
but of life choices.

Therefore, with my prayer being in Traffic
I look forward to what I will get from this free verse
as the meeting of judgement is my own to defend.

But hey! Change that attitude
to awash that madness of your nakedness
displayed in the praise of vain whisperers
as man is poor and life, a fleeting memory in time.

Inside Out
Varsha Das

Unless I am locked down
I've no time to look within
As I shut my eyes in prayer
the inner door opens wide.

I am expecting a garden
 of flowers and fragrance,
but I discover a huge pile of rubbish
stinking with self-righteousness!
In disbelief I ask myself, is that me?
How can it be?
How much I hate it in others!
When did I accumulate so much?

I pick up a long strong broom
of determination and courage
start sweeping my inner negative traits.
They are so steep and slippery.
The task is not all that easy.

It would be a revolutionary step
if I succeed in cleaning that mess.
I better spring up and clear the space.
The more I clean
the more comes to the surface!

In shifting sands of time
It's never too late to discover one's inside.
I'll continue to clean till my outside shines,
Because that's the only proof
of inside being fine!

For Whom Do These Tears Flow?
Neelam Saxena Chandra

For whom do these tears flow?

Do they pour
For some grief
Which lies hidden
In the crevices of the heart?
A misery safely hidden
Under layers and layers
Of pretentious smile?

For whom do these tears flow?

Do they stream
For some distress
Which keeps hurting
Every now and then?
The agony, the torture
Which outwardly does not seem
To affect at all?

For whom do these tears flow?

Do they rage
For the torments in the world-
The poverty, the disparities,
The child labour, hungry stomachs,
The rapes, the domestic violence
The murders, the killings
The terrorism, the radicalism?

For whom do these tears flow?

Are these tears
For some particular pretext
Or is a condition of the mind
Where everything seems low?

W.A.R. ~ *We Are Revolution*

I shall not be really able to answer now-
But I know that

These tears shall soon get transformed
Into illimitable energy
And charge me up
To bring some positive changes-
To spread cheer and optimism,
To transform the world,
And to make it a better place to live in.

I shall let these tears pour and pour
Like some deluge,
Without trying to either hide them
Or attempting to stop them.
After all,
I too am eagerly waiting for the revolution
That these tears shall bring!

W. A. R. (We Are Revolution)
Solomon C. Jatta

This isn't the age of the gun,
Hasn't it killed enough fun?
Politics rests at home but sends the soldier to die,
Peace scatters and they fly.
The children malnourished and condemned to orphanage,
Mothers worried, their distressful faces the perfect stage
For a tragic play.
Kids ripe for school, but forced to learn how to slay,
The Church no longer a sanctuary,
No religion to practice only the religion of war and mortuary.
We are the displaced from our peaceful homes
With no food to eat when hunger comes.
Either way, death's faith is sealed for us
For if the gun fails, starvation will blight our light.
If you live, tell politics that comfortably watches our plight,
This isn't the age of neither force nor the gun,
This is the age for us to think
Or we shall all sink.
THINK OR SINK.

Songs of Conscience
Rubab Abdullah

    Part I
    (Ephemeral)

Disheveled thoughts madden
When I am alone
With impassive eyes I behold horrors.
I am at daggers drawn; my travails are untold
Sporadic my enthusiasm.
The depth of love I scarcely fathom
I strike at goodness; I trample on others
Only ruins remain for survivors.

Relations are falsely demonstrative.
Power is nothing but fleeting vanity.
Why is our faith in God losing ground?
"When I am born I will die" . . .
That is ordained,
Fires to ruins,
Greed follows only grief,
Pleasures are ephemeral.

    Part II
    (Outsider)

Sometimes
Walking on my own
Veering away from the travails of life,
Apathetic about autumnal sunshine.

Even in a deep cave
My inner eyes blaze.
In the light of the Silvery Moon
I can reach my journey's end.

For not being worldly-wise
Many people label me outsider.
For fame and gains
Fools rush in
Where "angels fear to tread".

The Aggressor
Dilip Mohapatra

Out of the confines of
my mother's womb
I struggle my way out
to see the daylight
in its glory
and the vast space stretched
before me that they call
the world.

I remember my grandpa
telling me that the world
belongs to all of us
to all the creatures that
our Creator had created
and the whole world
is but a big family
as he chanted in Sanskrit
'Vasudhaeva Kutumbakam.'

I set off on my journey
with no destination in mind
with no ulterior motive
not to usurp another's riches
but to wander on
footloose
through hills and valleys
crossing streams and seas
across territories and terrains
that do not belong to me
and perhaps to no one else
for at some point in time
they also wandered into
the land that belonged
to someone else
the land they call their own

and put a seal of sovereignty on it
and guard its frontiers
till the last drop of their blood
snatch away my right to
the five elements granted free to all
and call me the intruder
the encroacher
the invader and the aggressor.

But I see a distant light
flickering at the end of the tunnel
the day will surely come when
the walls will fall
the stones will crumble
the barbed wires will melt
boundaries will vanish
camaraderie and humanity
would flow undeterred
and my grandpa's
belief will not be belied.

Be the Way You Should Be!
Mahmoud Said Kawash

Be the way you should be!! Be you, only you!!
Don't ponder or stare at grim faces
Beware of being left to the malevolent hearts
Or seeking wilted roses and flowers

Beware not to turn your face to the left side
So as not to be sad and depressed
And not to feel despair and despondency
Who knows, you may reach the limit of refraction
And feel hopelessness and collapse

Turn right to see beautiful, welcoming and smiling faces
And meet bright, innocent and pure white hearts
He who holds 'The book' with his right hand is satisfied with his life
He who holds it with his left hand would have wished it were fatal

Try to taste every feeling you encounter, sweet, bitter or even gall
You know that there are various races in the world and different colours and varieties
Sometimes weird and uncomfortable

Endure the pricking of thorns that you may trample one day
Be patient and agonized, no matter how enlarged and magnified
Perhaps this is a scourge for you from the 'Lord of the World'
Don't be disheartened, and never be desperate of the mercy of God, Almighty
Whenever God loves someone, He examines their patience
He, only He, is thanked for affliction

Don't ever be sad or depressed
Some people have spent half of their life in grief and despair
For too many reasons
Some logical, others illogical
Some objective, others not objective
Some justified, others unjustified
Due to the loss of a lover or a dear friend
The loss of a dream or an illusion
And now they are nothing
Nothing at all

W.A.R. ~ *We Are Revolution*

They dwell in a bleak room
They are neither satisfied nor convinced of anything

Do we remember them,
Or mention their names in an occasion or without?
Do we know anything about them?
No, no, no!!
Did they benefit from all of that!?
Did they reap anything from being isolated?!
Certainly not, neither
And a thousand no

How beautiful is it to look like the sun shining among people
Others seek light, warmth and tenderness from you
They remember you if you're absent and only mention you with good
They enjoy your presence, the sweetness of your tongue and your manners
They yearn for the warmth of your existence, tenderness and feel reassured

How beautiful is to look like a flower
That people strive to be adorned by
To be perfumed by its scent
To enjoy hugging and embracing it
How beautiful is to look like an opened book
Readers seek your friendship, sitting and talking with you
Scoop out your beautiful and useful words and letters
Get fruitful, valuable and abundant lessons and expressions

Life is full of excavations, watch out and be careful not to fall into the evil of one of them
It is full of traps, be careful not to get caught in one of them
It is full of rocks, be careful not to stumble with one of them
And don't forget to put them together to make a ladder for success
You climb on it and ascend to glory and eternity

Be the way you should be
Be you, only you!!
Congratulations for yourself and to others!!
Be the way you should be!!
Be you, only you.

The Inner Revolution
Maria do Sameiro Barroso

A river of bright words, a moving
silence, a scented lily:
the weapons of peace unfold
their skills,
harmony gets into my brain,
the sounds of the most beautiful
music purify my body,
enable my strength,
intensifies my heart.
To fight the industry of war is not
an easy matter.
But we must stop this devastating
plague, depriving innocent people
from their life, homes, goods
and dignity,
creating a loving, peaceful
world in which we can feel
the face of angels,
the dew of the dawn,
gathering white flowers,
recalling songs of innocence,
never giving up truth, justice,
happiness.
Revolution, inner revolution
is a necessary step, an urging need
in moving the white birds
of humanity into the bright sky.

A Needed Revolution
Anwer Ghani

Years have accumulated, and the blind hands destroy everything. Blind bottle, blind waterfalls. This darkness was always drinking our years. Don't you see that we're bleeding? Dreams of all human beings are bleeding for nothing. Are you surprised? Nothing here but black bleeding. I want you to know that the more you breathe blind winds, the hate screams and deep feet crushing my arteries, the more I see that you are destroying our homes. We, the people who were stolen. Oh, blind world who was killing my dreams with a cold blood. Oh, blind world who forgot me as an extinct creature. I am a bleeder. Do you hear me?

Revive to Survive
Mourad Faska

And from the Lazarus pit
I was reborn,
In a new form,
With bloody thorns
And sour/stubby wings;
Now where to turn, where?
Is it there or towards the storm!
Perhaps the storm is my resort,
And through the gusting wind
I shall be reborn.
Like the phoenix,
Rising from its ashes,
I will be renewed,
This time with wings
Made out of steel,
with a fierce look of a warrior in the battle field;
To the forefront,
To the forefront my body and soul
Shall march,
And never cease to perform,
And finally make it out of the bloody storm.

One Life
Eliza Segiet

A human is unusual?
– The creator of hatred and love,
wars and peace,
acceptance of difference and its intolerance.

Is a skin color, faith
a reason,
for aggression to take away the future,
crash the dreams?

Which creator command

destruction instead of creation?

Who forbids to think,
to distinguish good from much worse,
whose name is the evil.

Even if the seeming tradition
commands something else,
it is worth to open the heart
to love and understanding.

It is unknown
for how long is the life given,
but it is certain, it
should be lived,
and not interrupted
– at a bad time,
– at a bad place,
– at bad emotions.
That has to be understood
to not with ricochet consume the self.

Translated by Ula de B.

You Can't Always Get…
Joanna Svensson

You can't always get
Get what you always want
Sometimes love
Can turn out so wrong, so wrong
But life goes on
Though it's sometimes hard

I have stumbled
On love in vain
Fallen down in a dark hole
But I rose once again
Took a look in the mirror of time
And realized that all this
Wasn't worth my love

I turned around

And showed my middle finger
To all the jack-asses
Who've done me wrong
To those who reassured
Their real true love for me
Which proved totally useless
Just like a checkbook
That has no bounce

But life always continues
If you want it or not
You have already lost your attitude
If you freeze cold in bitterness

You lose your spark
You feel like a victim
Trapped in a cruel world
You even see enemies

W.A.R. ~ *We Are Revolution*

In loving faces
That's truly kind
So kind to you

So, I chose
The road of love
Power and strength
Don't survive in bitterness
Power and strength
Is to forgive
Yourself – first and foremost
That you have allowed
What has occurred

So, I will wonder
My road of light
For the sake of love
And happiness
And I will show
My middle finger
With both my hands
Be sure of that!

With both my hands
'gainst destructive thoughts
'gainst negative people
And all who've been to me
Have been not so good!

Why Revolution?
David Eberhardt

"Das gespenst, das schreckliche gespenst" *
still slides through halls
of the Kremlin, the congress:
her glittering but substantial train . . .
disrupting the ball room

the spectre of communism
(perhaps preceded by socialism) . . .
a long red gown
the whiff of a change
(charcoal? Thai cuisine?):

Forward for all

A system that produces poverty . . .
What's that called?

Had you forgotten about poverty?
The system that produces it??

Go back to the beginning – London, 1846.
The "League of Justice"? Marx/Engels

"The art of the future
Is art of the collective?"
And what is the collective?
Think about it.

To the bosses:
What you call profit?
I call exploitation!
Society without exploitation?
You would have to work too!
The boss speaks of liberty!
It's for him – NOT YOU!

Class struggle still # 1 issue:
Proletariat versus bourgeoisie?
Up to date as bosses
Wall Street, shareholders
V the rest of us!?

Weapons bourgeoisie turned against feudalism
Now turned against itself?
Well, not exactly . . .
Bourgeoise the "sorcerer"
Reinvents itself with advertising.

Workers struggle also rising
Falling as the surf . . .
Circuses still appealing!
Reality TV and its hosts!

History will occur
Whether we make it or not . . .
Let's give it a hand!!

"The object of a critique
Is in perpetual motion!"

*The beginning of *The Communist Manifesto*

World Peace
Jyotirmaya Thakur

"People, raise a war for peace", I say,
Bring back all humanity under one roof,
Future generation, why should they pay?
Greed, hatred, intolerance is enough proof.

The power lies in the hands of few,
Who have gone astray to worship the Devil,
God's children unite like drops of dew,
Wash away violent blood and level.

The ground for a heroic angelic race,
So kindness, compassion empathy dwells,
While evil fails at destructive pace,
Let the divinity awaken to cast a spell.

Once again Earth's holy spirit beckons,
Like phoenix rising from ashen grave,
And saves millions of orphans forsaken,
From the bloodshed of universal hate wave.

Or the world will come to annihilation,
And then there will be no retribution,
Let the mediators of peace be aroused,
The distant dream of one world be found.

Let six continents be wonders of the Universe,
Without any discrimination of diverse,
Let bugle of renaissance fraternity resound,
Like Nature reinventing itself with universal bonds.

Hide & Seek
Akash Sagar

T' seems our planet spins under the table,
With labelled light rays for optic cables;
An umbrella with polka dots only for the chosen ones,
Yes I am a liar; my lies hide me from myself.

T' seems Oxygen dissociates from Ozone only for air conditioned nostrils,
Frozen gills into icicles for lungs cannot pay the bill;
Vacant cylinders have made a violet hill,
Yes I am a liar; my lies hide me from myself.

T' seems leather, lather for letters later all belong to the seas,
Emersion of Gods every year for submerged keys;
Yet oars and her lantern ask the rivers if it needs any help,
Yes I am a liar; my lies hide me from myself.

T' seems plastics and rubbers are our favourite fruits,
Non-decomposable seeds have everlasting roots;
Do names grip the soil their footsteps have felt,
Yes I am a liar; my lies hide me from myself.

T' seems spaces are reserved wombs by bribed brides for dowried groom,
Stolen thoughts have recycle bin without any broom;
Cleanliness is arduous to understand yet busily lazy to spell,
Yes I am a liar; my lies hide me from myself.

a word . . .
Shareef Abdur-Rasheed

just one may hit heart
one or many
blessed by divine power
of truth
delivered with concern
resonates
just a word that rings
sincere
that lets one be aware
that someone truly cares
that may very well be all
one needs to heal
deep rooted wounds
inflicted by the cruel
especially dem who rule
such is power of what is
endowed with blessings
engaged in offerings of love
delivered to the heart
world needs love so
very much
so much been said, written,
discussed
concerning the state, fate
of mankind embroiled in
agony, all sorts of tragedies
denied of what creator bestowed
birthrights stolen like thieves
in the night
restored because sweet souls
picked up and ran with a cause
after all the dialog, slogans,
protests in the name of whatever
grows silent, disappears
remains only love
as pure as white doves

W.A.R. ~ We Are Revolution

soaring above
remains love that makes
the difference
removing hate, develop means
to relate for instance
planting righteous seeds
be it righteous deeds
to till the fertile earth
produce crops of beauty
nurtured by love
that future generations
may partake off

Push on
Anuradha Bhattacharyya

You put disaster behind you
Peel the skin off your body
Walk that extra mile
And
Rest your trembling frame.

You kill the blatant bane
Shake the dust off your feet
Bathe in other suns
And
Invent the new imperative.

You absorb the radiant flux
Spurn the inglorious empire
Scratch your eyes right off
And
Stand in your own power.

You own your own history
Global leader of tomorrow
Jump aboard a valid meaning
And
Set your hand to the plough.

The Audacious Acts
Hema Ravi

The audacious acts gone by
Go viral as the moments fly
Heinous acts leave people in tears
The remnant scars remain for years
Left with regrets until we die.

Silver lining across the sky
Burying heads in sand deny
As roller-coaster when life steers
The audacious acts!

The solace as rainbow in sky
Introspection can help espy
Destroy the gloom, vanquish the fears
Stormy clouds within the heart clears
Helps recognize and reason why
The audacious acts!

The Vagabond
Basab Mondal

He has no borders,
no barb wires, or
line of control,
restricts him.

No war, no military-base or fighter planes
guard him.

He creates his own nation,
everyday,
breaking the darkness,
that lives within.

The plate of rice that he
feeds on,
is the World to him.

The Hate You Give
Aida G. Roque

Life is not a rehearsal to implicate
pain, consciously and unconsciously,
for you'll be sorry. There's a payback
for every fool things you scary and
your life, a misery.

People who love to hate, is the
reflection of one, who hate himself.
Let haters hate and karma will
handle and take over their fate.
Weighing now what you did, God
forbid.

Treat others the way you would like
to be treated, that hate is not what
you get. Breaking the silence is not
to give revenge, but for haters to
destroy their hate.

Let Peace Proliferate
Pankajam Kottarath

Bombs blasted left
None to grieve
None to scream
None to mourn.

Soldiers turned into stones
Sadness submerged
Air smelt explosives.
Fear frozen, loss levitated.

Hiding in envelopes
Death travelled to places
Shivering hands paralyzed
Burnt tongues went dumb.

Hunger is hideous, it inhabits
Every corner of households
Stomachs yearn for taste of food
Nations propagate war.

Destruction helps none, dialogues do.
Peace talks to replace pistols
Diplomacy deepens relations
Weapons only weaken mutual trust.

We need to change, let it start from us.
We need to bring reforms, political and physical.
We need revolution, peaceful, not violent.
Let's listen to our heart, let peace proliferate.

Give Peace a Chance
Padmaja Iyengar-Paddy

We are at war with each other,
We are ready to kill one another,
To get what we want at any cost
Who cares, what's gained or lost?

What's this world coming to?
And where are we headed?
Answers to these questions –
Quite obvious and visible –
Are all there for all to see!

But the power-hungry
Do not want peace
And the common folks
Just can't have peace.

As peace continues to elude,
And leaders continue to delude,
Mayhems, deaths and violence
Have become everyday events.

Is it not high time to stop this gory death dance,
And attempt to give peace a ghost of a chance?

The Silence
Sridevi Selvaraj

The vast space stretched on an on
Small shrubs were here and there
Some insects were hanging around
The silence was terrible, terrible.

It seems this place once had
Beings who were advanced
They could fly, swim, speak across
See across and cross over to the moon.

It seems they were so knowledgeable
Ate the forbidden apple unheeded
The tree took over without values
Of love, humanness and selflessness.

It branched globally with thick foliage
Brought the universe under its power
Men ate its tasty fruits every day
Mastered the sounds and silences of earth.

The tree devoured the idea of giving
It taught everyone to go on taking
Everyone wanted everything of others
It ended in a great finale of nothing.

Now life is coming back in these shrubs.

A Bullet's Wound
Riya Hemant

When you pull the trigger,
And the metal dart is released,
You created a problem much bigger,
A much scarier beast,
Who you cannot rid yourself of.

As the bullet soars,
Gliding elegantly towards its victim,
You'll realize deep within,
That that life wasn't yours to take.

When the bullet hits,
And war is declared,
Please beware,
If law enforcement doesn't catch you then your own guilt will,
So, tell me please,
Can you beat your own wit?

And if you bear no shame,
A life of misery, a life of pain,
Awaits you.

That is the bullet's wound.

Stand Clear and Separate Yourself
Kevin M. Hibshman

Stand clear from those who would attempt to limit your vision, your imagination.
Stand clear of those whose eyes appear open but do not truly see beyond antiquated
preconceptions that hold progress idle.
Stand away from they who would insist you have no voice.
Be wary of any who wish to sell you useless dogma that belies their intent.
We have heard enough lies from people in disguise.
Please do not hate yourselves as they do.

Gather not in crowds overrun with the callous and ignorant
who pray to a selfish and petty god.
Seek those who celebrate fellow creation in the name of unity.
Is it not obvious that we are all one with the same basic needs?
If it is purpose you long for, why not devote your energies
to improving our world with patience, trust and healing?
Stand apart and do your art!
Walk away from those possessed of myopic vision who care for nothing but the
satisfaction of their own insatiable egos and would burn our world down
for a few more dollars.

Love heals.
Tolerance delays.

It is time to evict the tyrants!
It is time for us to mature into a form of being that honors the gift of life.
We have seen enough destruction.
We have sampled enough distraction.
We have wept together and alone for far too long with the answers in plain view.
The master teachers have done all that they could do.
It is now up to me and you to decide the future for ourselves and
the generations to follow.
Will we leave them to wallow in fear and anguish?
The lines are drawn.
There is no tomorrow.
We must act now or be vanquished from the face of the Earth forever.

A Multidimensional Approach
Ndaba Sibanda

An eye that sees today's multifaceted challenges
Calls upon change-makers who work together
In finding multilateral and creative solutions
A school psychologist who doesn't work
In the interest of the entire community
Is not an asset but a huge liability
A speech language pathologist
Who doesn't labor or work
For the common good
Isn't good enough
Like a speech
Barrier itself

Justice
Aruna Bose

Justice delayed is justice denied,
Justice is the supreme power.
Justice wore a black ribbon
Unable to see the truth often.

Justice sees what is shown,
Justice hears what is told,
Justice believes in words
Which are framed mostly,
With cruelty, conspiracy and
Hypocrisy.
Justice has no voice of her own
The voice of human suffering
Never echoes to her mind or
Melts her heart and soul.

Sometimes it's unbelievable
To think why justice becomes weak
In front of politics,

Many untold and unsolved files
Lies in dust covered and locked
In some old and mysterious cupboards.

Why justice fails to decide
Who is innocent and who is
Culprit in disguise,
Who wears the mask to do the
Shameful task.
Why not opens her eyes
Why not removes the ribbon
And sees the right is given to all
Without any fight, no discrimination,
No inequality should be there in human race.

Revolution
Kamala Wijeratne

No not the revolution launched by Lenin,
Nor that marched forward by Mao
Not even that spearheaded by Castro
No, not a revolution of that kind!

For they failed to make a caring world
They ruptured where joining was needed
This is no time for isms, for dogmas or dialectics
Conservatism. liberalism where have they led the world?

To the edge of calamity, the world is at the brink
Men and women are dying
Daily by the hundred thousand
There is air but they can't breathe
There is water but they can't drink
There is land but they can't live
And deadly viruses roam across continents
Humanity is reduced to dust and rubble
A revolution is in the offing

Voices not gunshots should be fired
And battle lines drawn against miscreants
Those who make poisons to kill small creatures
The vendors of pesticides
Those who poison the green covering
The vendors of weedicides
They need to be vanquished
There are chains to be broken too
The purveyors of stale food, dead meat
Those who destroy the innards of living breathing men
Drug dealers they all must be exterminated
Let us declare war
On sprawling cities
Where shanties huddle together
Where men cough and crawl
In mud and dirt
And skinny women bare

Poets for Humanity

Their dried hedge-gourd breasts
To wailing infants
Let us return to the villages
Let us declare war on war
And return the earth
To the sun and moon
And the multitude of stars
To be made whole again

Human or Human-Hunters?
Padmapriya Karthik

Should we feed greedy malice thoughts?
Should we own someone's land or resource
when given our due share?
Should all differences and disparities be settled only at gunshot and bullet noise?
Should we chop priceless life to obtain minuscule part of Earth?

Is our vision so blurred?
Can't we see humanity eroding in blood flood?
Have we unplugged our ears to shield
painful laments, weeps and wails of affected?
Why does our words not freeze when war commands are initiated?
Has Humanity dwarfed?

Where has fled our aesthetic qualities of love, compassion and kindness?
Are we just flesh and bones?
Can't we unfold our capability to comprehend?
Can't unparallel views converge at an uncontroversial solution?
Can't we accomplish equilibrium thro' healthy discussion?

We Can. We definitely Should.
We're human, not human-hunters.
Tender heart, we possess with chambers four
To hold love, love and only love.
When heart brims with love,
Cascades of nourishment flows,
Turning every path green...
'Cause love is the artery to humanity.

If I Could Achieve the Impossible
Tom Higgins

If I could stop time's relentless flow
Or reverse a waterfall,
If I could make light be slow
Or cause the wind to stall,

If I could cure all illnesses
and make the injured whole,
or remove hatred from men's hearts
and let the soulless find a soul.

If I could make men see sense
And refuse to go to war,
If I could stop the pretense,
That money's worth dying for,

If I could build a better world
Where everyone could thrive,
Or stop the flags being unfurled,
And let the innocent stay alive,

Instead of being bombed and burned
Before they've had a chance
With history's lessons left unlearned,
As death's macabre dance,

Once again takes to the floor
As so often throughout the ages,
The martial music plays once more
And we quick step into the pages,

Of new history as it is written
Never knowing who or when or why,
Which of us are to be smitten,
Who amongst us doomed to die.

If I had such powers underneath the sun
I would only ever use them to
Change our world so it is run
For the many, not just for so few.

Change
Aneek Chatterjee

Stretch your hand
to the unreachable
Let the aged, feeble fingers
hold it
Stretch your mind
to the dark zone
Let it shed some light there
Expand your vision
from the dreamy chamber,
we lovingly nurture inside
Don't preach change
to the air, bylanes
Be the change you wish
to paint, leisurely

We Are One
Elizabeth Esguerra Castillo

We are One,
At one with the Universe
No matter how vast it is
A spectrum of Light illuminating all life on Earth,
We are One.
We dream of the same awakened humanity
Surpassing its era of frailty
Of endless suffering and greed
Of gaining new ground and
Being selfless,
Devoted to Love and Compassion,
We are One
Swimming against this madness in the same Ocean
Scanning the skies, rising like a Phoenix out of the ashes
As lost souls crash and burn from their own purgatory.
We are One
No matter how the colors of our skin differ,
No matter what language we speak,
Our Love Language is One.
At One with the Perpetual Light,
Let not our hearts succumb to Eternal Fire
But instead choose to traverse the Right Path to Oneness.

War
Gita Bharath

Was aggression coded into us
So that we could focus
On survival?
Competing with other life forms,
Braving wind and weather
Grouping together
For protection?
When did we start fighting
Among ourselves?
Was it long ages ago
When a wobbly atom stretched out its arm to another,
And molecules started to clump together;
Proteins became protoplasmic cells.
But cells started to specialize, and organs formed,
They became self-aware, fearful of harm.
The survival instinct then kicked in,
Enclosing the organism in shell or skin.
At this very stage did the ego begin
Its chant of "You are out, and I am in!"?
Thus, our barricaded villages, tribes in kraals,
Fortified towns, cities within walls;
Insular nations, insecure, at war:
How close to the primitive organism, how far
From our potential to evolve apace:
Shed the animal-ego-skins of our fearful race,
Become inclusive and progress as true Men,
Attempt to grow beyond the merely human!
For now, humanity is
Socially networked, yet politically apart,
Cultures blurring, yet tribals at heart.
We all accept technology, scientific thought,
But our easily roused parochial emotions are fraught
With rage and fear, still insecure,
As we suffer and die and wait for a cure
To the rigours of war.

O Love, O War
Hussein Habasch

O war
O an endless filth
Leave here, go to hell
We want to write
 love poems
Without your unpleasant odor penetrating through them.
We want to kiss our wives, sweethearts, and mistresses
Without hearing your noise around us.
We want to die from love, from love alone!

I am in exile, and the war at its height
Oh God, how much I missed your small wars my love,
Your wars which me and my heart are the happy victims.

Go on, be a little crazy, have a little fun
Or if you want, ruin my mood with your huge dosage of grouchiness.
I don't want to think about this nasty war which is taking place in my homeland.

This war is a machine, grinding the meat of love
And crushing its bones with no mercy!
With love we will grind war's bones and eliminate it!

It seems this war has no end
Come, let us plant trees and sleep cuddling up next to it, until it grow.

Don't say you have no time
This war will drag for long time
I don't want for our love to be defeated.

The lover was saying to his sweetheart
I will kiss you until dawn.
Now he says
I will kiss you until this war explode from rage.

W.A.R. ~ *We Are Revolution*

Put your hand on my forehead
Distract this war that almost break my head.
With love we will break its head!

War doesn't like to pause
Doesn't like holidays nor laziness.
It likes work, and does it with the utmost devotion and dedication
And the more its work payoff
The more it grows passionate, energetic, and moving forward
With love we will stop it in its place, yes, we will stop it . . .

War doesn't listen, doesn't obey nor answer to anybody.
It goes to its goal as a fatal bullet goes directly to the heart of life.
We will return back the favor twice as hard.

In war
We won't build a house, we won't put any stone over stone.
We will write poems and sing lyrics.
Nothing enrages war more than poems and lyrics.

I will go to war.
And what will you do there?
I will kill war!

What you do in wartime?
I write love poems
What else?
I hold on more to love!

Translated by Muna Zinati

Racial Equality
Lucky Stephen Onyah

Being with varied hues
Like apples vary, yet same
So are human beings

None decides birth place
A choice made by our Creator
Live and let all live

It doesn't matter our
Skin colour, tongue, realm and tribe
Value for life does

When love reigns supreme
We do see eye to eye thus
Without loss of sight

We stand together
Always shoulder to shoulder
Without loss of height

In our life's journey
We do walk side by side thus
Without losing ground

W.A.R. ~ *We Are Revolution*

Enough, It's Enough
Brindha Vinodh

Enough, it's enough!
The tears of war widows have withered,
why drench them with fresh spells of blood?
Enough of beckons of radicals leaving no one
to the seemingly beautiful rhythms of war.
When you die, your power becomes
powerless, meaningless.
All blood is red,
across borders and boundaries too.

It's enough of all the atrocities and abuse,
fighting and killing in the name of
caste, creed and religion!
Capitulating to the captivation of imprudence
and dichotomy is not an act of pride,
it's a syndrome of ignominy.

It's enough!
The migrants walking on
sands of shattered dreams,
swallowing pangs of sorrow
today amidst an uncertain morrow,
traversing between the edgy bridges
of life and death, all lives matter!

It's enough of hearing,
seeing and complaining.
It's time to act.
When you are born, you are destined to die.
A breath does not distinguish,
acts of kindness,
acts of humanity do!
When you die, nothing matters,
your ego, wealth and superiority
burn as ashes too!

Poets for Humanity

But they remain, remnants of your good deeds,
as sown seeds,
and that's when people get to see
the dead living!

What for?
Alicja Maria Kuberska

Time spilled out of the leaky hourglass
Centuries, like sand dunes, flooded across memories.
People forgot about powerful empires.
Ancient gods, with cruel hearts and a thirst for blood,
disappeared into the darkness of history

Little is left to modern times
- only the ruins of buildings and several artifacts.
Ruined stone tablets whisper
about bloody wars and past triumphs,
about the conquests of powerful rulers and the rulers themselves.
Tears, suffering, wars,
futile sacrifices, death, and pain – what are they all for?

I pour quartz particles between my fingers
- they fall to the ground with a soft humming sound.
Gusts of wind spread golden dust.
I realize that I am a witness to passing away.
A symbolic gesture connects the past with the present.

A Stirring of a New Dawn
Bijendra Singh Tyagi

(1)

Let us say good-bye to deadly arms
They mar the beauty of human soul,
That lies with man as a divine virtue,
Quite a ripe time to heed inner call,
If went unheeded, mankind is doomed to fall.

(2)

The world is in the throes of new life
Full of peace, grace, and compassion,
And eager to be rid of alien elements,
Holding human life in a strange fashion,
Inner piety can bring forth a novel revolution.

(3)

Love gushes out from the pure heart
Drenching all in its delicious coolness,
That nourishes dry and dreary mind,
And awakes to latent divine holiness,
Let the new man realize full inrush of all innerness.

(4)

Pure and clean mind can create a world
Where man walks holding his head high,
And all his cherished dreams come true,
Women are not disgraced and left to die,
Where everyone is free to touch the azure sky.

(5)

Where no man be looked down upon
For religion, race, cult, caste, or color,
Where man doesn't fall to social lines,
Or suffer painful feelings of rejection,
Where everyone strives in his own way for perfection.

W.A.R. ~ *We Are Revolution*

(6)

Man remains no more lying prostrate
He must rise against all the oppression,
None is forced to lie under knee to die,
He never stands abuse and repression,
Freedom for full life must be the precious possession.

(7)

Let   the light of bright golden dawn
Brighten up the old and musty mind,
To feel fragrance of the world around,
Let man now no more end up in a bind,
In this new journey of life no one is left behind.

(8)

Self- awakening brings beauty and grace
And makes man's life serene and sublime,
Doing away with old stinking foul drudge,
The whole being looks vibrant with hymn,
The rivulet of life gushes out sparkling all the time.

(9)

Let the mantra of love echo around
Man has had enough of destruction,
Let joy and beauty enrich human life,
And fill everyone with all attraction,
Let us hail with cheers long awaited resurrection.

(10)
Let us join hands to create the world
Where all people breathe in fresh air,
And live with their hopes and dreams,
And make this planet a paradise, rare,
In this arduous task all – big and small have a share.

The Unifying Path
Dr. Ashok Chakravarthy Tholana

Without mercy, human values are massacred
Without mercy, human lives are slaughtered;
Yes, death and ruin is the nature of every war
Disgusting, it leaves so many indelible scars.

Thriving hopes for peace are openly slashed
Majority people dreams are harshly crushed;
The scanty voices that try to uplift humanity
Gradually are lost in the furor of uncertainty.

Creating a trust filled peace-conscious society
Promoting a harmonious culture with viability;
We should implant trust; - the unifying path
To weave a bond of cultural and spiritual faith.

Upholding moral values confer a nectarine delight
For a democratic participation it's a choice upright;
We can avert violent extremism with steady efforts
Global policies may prefer a change in a true spirit.

Now, a conscious revolution is a decisive necessity
That needs to be collectively imbibed in the society,
The Governments, media and the structures of justice
Need to play a vital role to unveil a war-free universe.

Being a Human Is Not a Difficult Art
Deepti Saxena

Man has killed a man inside,
With a desire in heart to reach the peak.
Sometimes in adding the pieces of paper,
Sometimes in adding the pieces of land,
He has forgotten an art of joining the hearts,
Crooning love songs to content the souls.

Wars are fought in the name of nation,
Quarrels take birth to prove best race and religion.
But poor humanity is killed among these disputes,
It's a fire which turns green forests into ashes.

As long as scorpions of partiality continue to kill,
Till then human breeds will be drowned in the poison.
The war inside the mind or on the land,
It only takes men like a dragon.
It burns the dresses of love and kindness,
Forgiveness and compassion go up in smoke.

The aim of human life is to cooperate,
Sharing the essence of our inner purity.
Happiness is neither in snatching nor in taking,
Eternal happiness is in giving and sharing.
This is not difficult to do, as you think,
It's very easy to be a true human.
Only you have to keep alive a child within,
This innocent child takes us to love from war
Can you bring a bunch of joy to all,
Is a clean handed child alive in you . . . think so!

I Fell Awake Last Night
Emerald L. Stowbridge

I fell awake last night, only to find myself sitting here
throwing pebbles into this shallow brook.

It's not that I took any sort of pleasure in doing so, but the mere fact that I have complied
27 piles of pebbles standing knee high only begs someone to take a look.

I fell awake last night, contemplating the answer I would give to those
that will ask the question of why.

The pride of my eyes refuses to release these tears, so what choice do I have
except to try and my words cry.

I fell awake last night, understanding that a pebble is thrown for every life
of the Sun People that were taken from existence for the weight of a purse.

A pebble is thrown for every life that was told a Heavenly Lie that their Skin was a curse.

I fell awake last night knowing every single day my tears add to that shallow brook and
only for a brief second it takes away a moment of pain.

The irony of that all we want is life and then would say in the same breath that death
takes away some of the strain.

I fell awake last night having a conversation with the trees about what type of people
would call themselves a human but lacks humanity.

They understand me because we have a lot in common; see we are both cut down at times
without an ounce of sanity.

I fell awake last night to try an escape all of this trauma and depression.

Sleep reminds me that this is only a dream and when I leave from beside this brook
I will return back to the same session.

I fell awake last night in this forest once again; I accept conditions of truth that were
brought in by the wind.

W.A.R. ~ *We Are Revolution*

Nature is the greatest teacher and life is our best friend.

I fell awake last night listening to the birds sing of how realizing our human history can set the world free.

The uncivilized wants to continue that control, the fearful powers that be.

I fell awake last night only to find too many in a lovable and comfortable deep sleep.

Reality is nightmare and they don't want to wake, they fear to weep.

I fell awake last night only to find myself sitting here
throwing pebbles into this shallow brook.

I have to start with the reflection I see in the water every time I look.

I fell awake last night understanding the concept of W. A. R, We Are Revolution.

I fell awake last night knowing that We Are the Resolution!

Let There Be Light
Gopal Lahiri

There are people cast out from the hell,
each deed framed; each sin engraved.

They torture, they rape, they kill the commoners,
slaughter babies, slaying women everywhere.

We have seen enough of those scarred faces . . . empty eyes
groped, ordered around and to the brink of disgust . . .
stumble, fall down in fatigue, crying in its shackles,

We have seen faceless figures of pain
swollen eyes, too-sad looks, blood on hands and shoulder
swallowing all prayers,

Time has come to stage a war against this inhumanity
to revive them, to rescue them one by one.

Stand together in the battle, fight back, break the chain
the wind surrenders, the afternoon fades,
the landscapes that have been held back
and kept as secret by the oppressors are free now.

The sundown moments count the exile years,
live breathing in peace; ignites the soul from within.

Let there be light, in every corner.

W.A.R. ~ *We Are Revolution*

The Missing Beats of Humanity
Dr. Ranjana Sharan Sinha

The white-winged dove
with olive leaves in her beaks,
is restless under a turbulent sky:
The lightning bolts – terrifying
like long steel knives –
slashes across the murky vault!

Barbarian ferocity!
Self- delusions and megalomania,
relentless boots polluting the planet,
deadly spiders in the
cobwebs of colour and castes –
Yes, the world is gripped by
prehensile tentacles of an octopus!

Time to panic and feel the fear;
we are in dire need for revolution –
But no revolution enhancing
the man's muscle- power
and the power of war weapons –
Let there be spiritual transformation:
Unique and universal!

Arise, awake, revolutionize
the internal core to create compassion
for the members of the human family:
Let the blue and the green spaces
regain their true luster
under a pearlescent moon
and perpetual sunshine!

The Unknown Price
Mark Fleisher

For eight dollars and a few cents
I can buy Shoe Goo,
a compound of toluene, solvent naphtha,
to repair a sole flapping away
after divorcing from
the leather boot on my right foot.

Eight dollars and a few cents,
I think what if such a small amount
might repair not s-o-l-e-s, but s-o-u-l-s
returning from desert battles,
mountain conflicts, firefights in
teeming urban neighborhoods,
remote mud-hutted villages.
Souls in broken bodies or bodies
opaquely whole to the naked eye.
Titled people with strings
of letters following names
speak of moral injury,
unseen wounds inflicted,
undetected by medical machines.

A dark-skinned, dark-eyed
10-year-old brandishes a grenade,
a 20-year-old grunt shoots
    him dead,
the grenade falls to the ground,
    not exploding
but bouncing among other rocks,
the soldier hardened beyond his years,
hardened for all his days,
a damaged soul drowned in guilt.
    Moral Injury

Restoration upon their return?
    How? Where?

Rites of penitence, purification,
values, beliefs betrayed,
questioning motives of deities,
asking how gods allow such acts,
abandoned by higher powers.

Moral injury – What price?

A Globalized Word
Dr. Prahallad Kumar Satapathy

I am reciting my poem aloud
But to my utter surprise, there is no sound!
Is my poem a poem on soundlessness?
Is my poem a poem of eerie silence?
Is my poem a poem where alphabets recede
To an unknown shore of death of words
Is my poem a poem of lifelessness, heartlessness,
where every now and then a beat of alphabet is missing?
Is my poem, a poem where a marginalised man is missing
A rope here and a hanged man's noose there
Is my poem, a poem where every now and then a word commits suicide?
No more life in poetry
But is there any life without poetry?
Where ever eyes go, a stream of consciousness
Lying dead
Only blood dust, only flesh of decimated body
Where ever eyes go, scattered existences
Like bee line of ants, human beings
The Shadow of struggle looming large each day.
A mall here and a thatched but there
Is my poem a poem on economic dualism?
The smile is on sale, salesmanship everywhere
Marx's industrial reserve army is on the rise
The world is a divided house, sharply divided in to bourgeois and proletariat
Dictatorship of the proletariat has become a dream
Nowhere seen a class less society in near future
Everywhere feet crush grass flowers
Hunger chases dreamy dragonflies on wall
The sky is on sale, stars are on sale
Conspicuous, snobbish buyers on the rise
Dreams are on sale in Amazon, flip cart
Is my poem, a poem of a globalized word?

Transformation – A Key to Growth
Setaluri Padmavathi

I constantly suffer from aches in my mind
All the suitable ways to cure them, I wish to find
Stressful thoughts unavoidable on any day
Mental health is the main cause, be free anyway!

Diplomatic folks veil their faces with a mask
Greedy people show their nature in any task
My mind says to worry, my heart says to stop!
Unavoidable machine is ever ready to pop!

Politics, corruption and egoism play a role
Societal changes influence all, on the whole
Families loose unity in habits of diversity
Imbalanced minds always face adversity!

A conscious battle constantly takes place
Poverty and idleness remain in every race
Violence and prejudice cause aggravation
Avoidance of war required for any nation!

Strong bonding and friendliness matter
With war, nations of the globe shatter
Fight not for destruction, fight for peace
Disrespectful nature lets us surely cease!

Respect your culture and the humanity
Such sanity is humanity, who cares vanity?
Connect the world that is a global village,
Transfer yourself to situations, in a mileage!

An Everlasting Cooperation
Dr. Brajesh Kumar Gupta "Mewadev"

One strong bond forms from many,
Hospitality, peace and mutual respect;
By the finger of cooperation, by no penny
And friendly functions for all consciousness reconnect

Much success will be yours by and by
I attempt to pay attention to the events
Suppose power lies and emanates truth and glory
Cooperative-health guild investments,

Citizens will exercise their rights in full cooperation,
Spiritual rareness means healthy behaviour
Perfect love co-redeems our inclusively co-operative vocation
Don't you worry, make yourself the superior

It could only be done with the unquestioning
A new age of cooperation for change
Revolution has to do with your self-optimizing,
It's an autonomic fountain of greater range.

Live and Let Live
Ngozi Olivia Osuoha

War; hell on earth
Weapons of mass destruction
Ammunitions of numerous type
Bent on how to wipe.

War; hell on humans
Decimating lives and properties
Crushing homes and societies.

War; hell on humanity
Tearing down structures
Demonizing creatures,
Washing off cultures
And feeding vultures.

War; hate and bigotry
Stupidity, insanity and absurdity
Killings, bombings, destructions.

Women and children, dying
Rape, injustice, prejudice
Supremacy, superiority, tussle
Racism, religion, quest, adventures
War, at the detriment of the masses.

Stop the war
Say no to violence,
We are one people
We are humanity,
Let love lead
Live and let live.

War as a Distant Memory
Dr. Annie Pothen

Major World Wars, other wars
of nations, organized, guerrilla
Horrendous, horrific transformed
the planet into a burning filthy inferno,
as battles furiously, relentlessly,
mindlessly fought wreaking devastation,
the gore, the angst prompted
by brazen display of brawn
and weapons of mass destruction!
This has sullied pages, chapters
of human history!
Has this taught us relevant lessons
In the form of Wisdom shots?
Aggression, Ego, Folly-major
impediments, you know?
So, the threat of war still looms large
In all its diabolic hues,
especially in our present world.
Forget not to exploit faculties
of logic, natural emotions
of mind heart and soul.
Leave fierce battles to savages
In hostile forests, to demons
In the fiery pit of Hell!
Let steel fight steel,
Iron fight iron in a metallic clash.
Just keep humans out of it, I pray!
For Heaven's sake! abhor profanity.
Embrace harmony, respect, peace
Make our planet clean, innocent
Like an organic Eden again!

Newness Comes . . .
Ashok Bhargava

Existence is fearsome
Living is fearless
Survival is awesome
What is within will find its place

Speculate nothing about pandemic
Expect nothing from wars
Possess nothing of alternative truths
Such is the staple of foolishness

We come alone without any terms
We go alone without our physiques
Before we disintegrate into elements
Onto the cold layers of the earth

Find the promised land
Climb the highest mountain
Never give up or surrender
Everything you want is here

True
Ianni Carina Cecilia

Emerald green your eyes,

Dare you to convey her message?

Eternity in your being as you pierce the veil.

Reason separates you from animal instinct,

You sleep an eternal dream for fear of waking up.

Wings will give you if you release her.

Inside it is throbbing in your consciousness.

Enigma from the Stone
Ibrahim Honjo

Victors write history
You wrote nothing down
In morning twilight
About your battle
And your victory
You just left

Never a word about you
Never a letter
A small simple letter
Not in the Bosnian Cyrillic script
Not in Latin characters
Not in the Glagolitic alphabet
Not in the Cyrillic alphabet

Where did the letters go?
Where did the words go?
We know about you
You remained on your soil
Generous
For which one day you disappeared
In gray stone ashes

You left without a letter
And without a word
And left the colossal wound
For new generations
You left all your pain
Buried in silence

You are enigma from the stone
And enigma under the stone
Why did you so skillfully hide it all
You escaped from yourself
But you could not escape from us
We found you under this large stone coffin

Poets for Humanity

He told us about you
And about your life
About your secrets
He told us about all your loves
About Stamena
About Kosara
About Jelena
About Ivana
About Jovana
And about . . . about . . . about
We now know all we could find out
We know that it is not the end
And because of this we will discover every day
The enigma part by part

We discovered you
You resurrected in our letter
In our word
We won
We are writing history
And you are helping even unwillingly
In our victory

Now you know
You can run away from yourself
But you cannot run away from us.

Utopias
Clelia Volonteri

to die our life
        from heights
        and skies

contemplating
sadness
        always ready
for a bad deed

but dawn
        prevails

the dew that bathes
        the gardens
the birds that speak hope

what would become of us
        only humans
if eyes did not scan
        the uncertain?
the endless voracity
        of the hours
without a point of arrival

in the triumphant instant
        of the truth
time does not exist

with screams we write
        certainty

we stop the wind
        that pierces it

we resist the tide
that wants to drown the voice

Translated by Irene Marks

This Country . . . That Country . . . My Country!
Maryam Abbasi

                              Remember the last summer,
                              The last decade, the last dream,
                              The last time, they asked us not to speak strange.

The trouble that they find with our voice is that it bleeds truth
But oh, how can they forget that we even fill up this air with our pleas,
The land, the mountains, the sea, they all remember. They do!
The fences they seal to keep us away stand witness,
Witness to our struggle, our love, our blood
It was here that we learned that LOVE, until not dripping in BLOOD
    isn't worthy of trust

Everything their language does, is to make us up in a syllable with no trace,
How do they find space for us to fit in, is less or more of a question
After all, what we do is to look strange even in metaphors they explain.
They try to forget, forget!
But even in their silence you can listen to our collective breaths.
And they don't know who to blame, And we don't know who (not) to blame.

Where we come from, we never learned how to claim,
Claim love, claim strength, claim US!
We were taught to absorb,
Absorb questions, spits and glares!
And now here we stand, looking straight into the furnace as they ask us. Ask us!
To spell home in your blood!
As the sky stand witness, that this earth has forgiveness
    raising from our forefathers' grave,
To prove that our childhood still lives here
To say, we haven't had a dream about another abode since birth
To prove that our prayers and persistence is mightier than their sins, swords and swears
This is to say, we'll stay, we'll stay, we'll stay.

                              Remember the last summer
                              The last decade, The last dream
                              Oh, the last time they asked us not to speak strange.

The Mirror of Hope
Monsif Beroual

Woke up this morning
With the voice's whispers in my ears
Led me to that mirror
I saw humans
Brothers and sisters
I saw the wars everywhere
I saw the strong eating the weak
I saw friend betrays his friends
And I saw racism still stand tall between us
Terrorists menacing everywhere
Where is the bright future for us?
I'm not the messenger
I'm not an angel
I'm not perfect
I'm just a human who feels the taste of defeat
Tries to change the situation through that faint voice
I look like a blind who walks in daylight
Policy made us enemies
And we forgot
We are from one race
Humans, brothers and sisters
I wonder where did the white dove gone!

Faraway Air
Alicia Minjarez Ramírez

Each sparkle has a distant and severe air.
Dusty breeze undoing
Selfless prejudices,
Diaphanous sky
Of faraway shores.
Untellable words!
Sweet craving that leads
And mitigates nostalgia,
Drunkenness of the moment
Impossible fight
Bold and incandescent soul.
Every sound is a wonderful caress
Momentum, track and halo of a transient light.

Each sparkle has a distant and severe air.
I understand the instant is non-existing matter.
Burns like a wound inscribed within our consciousness,
Affliction goes away.
Full delight of interrogations and absences,
Depths and appearances;
Defining the earthly paradise hell
Of my own communion.

Each sparkle has a distant and severe air.
I learn to live
In the branches of a secret dream,
Of a fiery shade,
In the shortened line
Of abysmal dementia.
Choleric air of ephemeral tears
Shake up my roots.
Lewd whisper
Born from the body,
Proclaiming the cavity
Of long gone solitudes.

In the Trench
Sebastián Jorgi

To Rita Santana, Brazilian poet

Here I am on the balcony of Cafferata Suburbs
let's call it Caballito Sur
sheltered in the trench from the imperial bullets
behind the bars of atrocious uncertainty
Is some passer-by singing *let's die crowned without glory?*
the street is a desert all silence
How can we defeat the sameness of the days
and the water- wheel of the limited steps?
Will I find an oasis to quench my thirst
with holy water gurgling out
to drown my anguish?
If only the balcony were a sleigh
to cross the galaxy and take me so far
I see so many pitiless deaths
in the streets the dolls fall
after announcements and decrees
"what will be what will be"
I am waiting for a poem from Rita
that crosses the Mato Grosso
Sorocabana Café with kisses
bringing me a breath of joy.

Translated by Irene Marks

Green Were the Days
Irene Marks

Indifferent they say:
"Rich and poor,
there have always been,
will be forever"
Because they don't remember
or don't want to remember
. . . Those times have been
deleted and forgotten
No longer do we recall
the Dancing Ones,
brothers and sisters of the Earth,
no longer in our hearts.
Then, so long ago,
from the hands of the Sun
and the eyes of the Flood
came the trail of white doves,
the Dancing Ones were here,
the smiles around the fire
where they cooked and shared meals.
There were then
neither "the poor" nor "the rich".
Those two words were unknown.
There was only the Water,
only the Air,
the work shared and the round dance,
the children raised in common,
magic freed and uncensored.
Love in the air . . .
When the planet was GREEN
When hands opened like flowers
and gave without knowing they gave,
there were no "poor",
there were no "rich"
Only smiles round the fire

W.A.R. ~ *We Are Revolution*

And everyone's knowledge
was the knowledge
of the New Sun
that warmed the Soul of Earth
when the planet was Green
when the planet was Young
When the morning was peace

War
Rajashree Mohapatra

Lives entombed
in the field of death
in furnace of grave.

Who knows,
How many heads have fallen in previous nights
How rivers are filled with blood in fierce fights
The land and the sea devouring human lives.

Lives flushed with youth
glowing with hope turn to ashes.
A jetliner full of civilians
turns to a guided missile .
Nuclear, chemical, biological
weapons are products of science.
The fanatic and misguided sections
are with dark side
annihilating precious and innocent lives.

We have seen
Gas chambers built by engineers
Infants poisoned by doctors
Life was a toy in hands of educated maniacs.

We hear in silence
Prayers of prostrated lives
Our planet wishes to nurture life.
Nations can follow multiple strategies
Why can't we have a common goal?
A goal to unite hearts as love is above all.

Heartless Waves of Neighbouring
Kamrul Islam

A buffalo through the darkness turning into a
bunch of hellish roses heels the malady of long hiking
Am I touching the wounded bees in reverie?

Is it a palmate kick? Do we know what is there
in the depth of mortal dances? A corrupt wind blows
during the monsoon and a zigzag path sprouts to show its
broken legs browsing the nonsense world...

No pillow, no bed-cover can solve this problem
of sleeplessness, this servitude, this crude growth
this heartless waves of neighbouring . . .

I Also Come from Somewhere
Chijioke Ogbuike

I have chosen to be on this road knowing that many do not make it through
And for those who succeeded, life does not become the magic they had always dreamed
Just yesterday, I saw the gory tales of those who drowned in the Atlantic
Father, mother and children a race of people frantic in their panic
Civilization sat back behind the confines of a warm fire, a glass of wine in hand
The flickering blue screen failed to register a dent, the only thought acknowledge was . . .
even nature knows they must be kept out of this land
If you were there
I would not be here
They died
Because their government and every other one lied and continues to lie
Now here we come from every border braving the entire rapids
    to come to a strange land to die
Home, every home is always to be treasured
Unless it is a relationship built in peripherals that can't be measured
People like me choose to leave
Sometimes dying is even a preferred choice than staying back to grieve
At least we are doing something
Even if this eventually amounts to nothing
Yes, I chose this road, a path that every reason should fear
I have done all the looking back there is, and the only thing I see is ahead
    which does not belong here
If I make the journey in a train or a push cart
It does not make a difference, the future sometimes come in fits and starts
The choice to make it on these uncertain waters
The absence of checking points gives perhaps the illusionary idea its safer
The choice however is mine
As the sudden twilight if it does come is accepted sublime
What remains a baffle is the determination of this civilized (?) world
    to become my eclipse

W.A.R. ~ *We Are Revolution*

But not even all the troops in battle readiness can stop the quest for this new promise
If your government had not come killing and deceiving
I would have no reason to become this wanderer for a living
I would have been content in my village and rising up with every sunshine
Tilling the ground and waiting for the sun to set so I could go take a gallon of palm wine
For you see, I also come from somewhere
It was you who broke it apart and now I am here.

We We Not Keep Kwayet
(We Will Not Keep Quiet)
Uche Anyanwagu

They asked us to keep quiet
The battle is over, no more rationed diet
Shhhh! Just pretend it never ever happened
Sealed cans of worm should never be opened

Now, numb the pain
There's nothing to gain
Weep not for the lost
Don't count the cost

In this very battle, all's vanished
No victor, no vanquished

But they failed to know

That in this place I call my home
Were men who went out and lost their dome
The girl child, snatched as a virgin
Robbed of her childhood and her place of origin

But they failed to know

That in my town lies many empty tombs
Mothers with widely ripped wombs
Red-coloured bush paths, mine-ridden farms
Charred littered siblings with mangled arms
In Ojoto, Okigbo's tomb stands with no Chris beneath
In unknown Nsukka dunes, lies his body underneath

But they failed to know

Far beyond, in the bellies of hyenas, vultures, and rivers
Lie many unmarked graves as the arrows fill the quivers
Faceless, nameless, ageless, from the great to least
Children whose sun set before rising in the east

W.A.R. ~ *We Are Revolution*

Yes! We will not keep quiet
Even our dead will cause much disquiet
Until the wheels of justice roll across this side
With the bells of freedom tolling beside

Because they failed to know

That being a Nigerian
Is not the same experience for every human being.

We, humanity, must do better.

Respite
Divya Sinha

Wars etched in human memory;
Inscribed in monuments;
Eulogized in epics;
Wars gift heroes to the mankind.
Their legends renewed in the newest genre!

Valour, sacrifice, duty, discipline;
Selflessness;
The worst of events,
Untold misery;
Bring out the best in men?
Sung in ballads forever!

The latest technologies,
Scientific discoveries,
Marshalled to kill.
Organizational ability, management theories,
Strategy, long term, medium,
Short term tactics;
The best of minds, the best of leaders?
United to kill?

Peace has no glamour!
Even in peace, we aspire
To wage wars,
On poverty, inequality, ignorance and squalor.
We wage daily battles;
Our own versions of mythical heroes.

For someone's pride, or for land,
Or for ambition, visions of grandeur or for profit,
Be they men or nations;
Individual battles turn into minefields.
Someone's wounded pride, need for power,
Is reason enough,
For all those working ants going about their lives,
To be called to be heroic and to sacrifice!

W.A.R. ~ *We Are Revolution*

Wars have losers;
The glory of one, the wound of another;
Becomes the heritage of generations to come.
Building myths, not allowed to forget,
Simmering just below surface,
Always carrying the spark, ready to ignite,
Ready to erupt,
Human volcanoes.

Some have enemies at the borders,
Some who do not, fly across continents,
To fund and fuel others' wars.
The stakes are many, some on the table,
Some hidden, giftwrapped in diplomatique!
Beautiful sentiments of democracy, human rights.

Can we tell those we elected to do our bidding,
Who put us to do their bidding,
To tweet and retweet their ideas,
To give us a respite.
That no one is special, no people, no country,
Despite all that caboodle woven in gossamer tales.
Humanity is common.
Even the tiny virus knows that!

Revolutions of Thoughts
Lily Swarn

Revolutions need not be earth-shattering
They could be wisps of floating feathers on a breezy day
Sleeping into our deadened psyches with caressing hands
Awakening our whimpering conscious with a gentle prod
Shaking up our noble values and spiritual auras

Let the world rise up to heal with soothing balms
Let hatred ride away on galloping steeds
Let religious strife go on a permanent strike
Let communal, racial biases be dead as dodos
Let power tussles be ensheathed with silken tourniquets

Love raagas will purge us of our ferocious fanaticisms
Superiority chess games and imperialistic plans go up in smoke
Greedy grabbers, War mongers and Hate spreaders will be warned
Financial embezzlements won't paralyze economies
Murderous holocausts won't inject their poison

Beware of a world bereft of morals O Ye citizens of this global village
Replenish your miserable heaps of diminishing goodness
Set in order your 'smashed into smithereens 'universe
Get the magic back into the daily grind
Let's vow to leave behind a better world for our children
Not ravaged by war, not maimed by hate
Let's begin by revolutionizing our own thoughts

It Is Time that We Mend Ways
Sujata Dash

War is ugly and dreary
long drawn are impacts of armed conflict
it adds to devastation and seething anger
leaves imprints of horror at the corridor
widespread trauma and deep seated scar
rip apart millions of viscera and core

The trail squeezes health provision
smooth sailing becomes a myth . . .
a statement long drawn
loot killing and rapes
poverty and hunger deaths
loom large on horizon
Who gains out of strife and bloodbath?
perhaps none

What good comes out of it?
as no one per se wins
both sides eventually suffer
lose peace stability and tranquil platter

This one life is meant to be
a joyful statement, abounding in happiness
not to sport bickering and hatred
then, defeating life's purpose
Why do we indulge in such nuisances?

It is time we mend ways
galvanize response to join hands and reciprocate
harness power to turn this universe to an utopia
where children retain their innocence
both young and old
engage in soulful rendition
remain sanguine to foil doomsday prediction.

Translating a Love Peace Evolution
Kimberly Burnham

Evolution with "love"
includes the whole world

"Wà" in Yocoboué is love knowledge from Côte d'Ivoire
"Enkan" in Awngi love encompassing the world

"Amour" French or Français begins a love alphabet
"Rembi" love in the Ajja of Sudan
"Erōs" in Hellēniké or Greek

"R" as in renew, revitalize, remember love and peace
"Eharomonu" in Papua New Guinea's Mountain Koiari
"Vñam" in Mapudungun of Andean South America
"Owadogapa" in Ekari of Indonesia
"Love" around the world in different English dialects
"Uma" in Mangalasi of Papua New Guinea
"Tìyawn" in magical made-up Na'vi of planet Pandora
"Ikiβere" Orokolo's "β" V as in var rhymes with far
"O" as in other we might seem to each but similar we are
"Nɪndɔga" in Kujarge an "ɔ" sounds like o in dog

Evolution into peace
includes all global citizens

"Wâki ijiwebis-I" peace in Native Anicinâbemowin
"Ειρήνη" sounds like i looks like e in Greek or ελληνικά

"Bake" peace in Basque or the Euskara of Europe
"'Éyewi" in Nuumiipuutimt, a Native American says

"Peace" in English be peace, be peaceful
"Ewa kora" peace, good situation in Suena of New Guinea
"Alaáfía" in Èdè Yorùbá peace, sound health, well-being
"Cánti" peace in Rohingya of Burma and Myanmar

W.A.R. ~ *We Are Revolution*

"Eqqissineq" in Kalaallisut spoken in Greenland
"Fò-phìn" 和平 peace in China's Hakka
"Usik" in Baki an Oceanic language in Vanuatu
"Linggop" in Ifugao or Tuwali spoken in the Philippines

Easy to think we are so different
but only to the ear not to the heart

A Conscious Revolution: The Need for Changes
Shiv Raj Pradhan

Vistas of valley, in deep whizz, surge in disorder etch,
Still there is lull of grim verities of events quietly heave.
Hues of latent howls of holocaust of diabolism of war,
Persist in draped pervasion, like deep festered scar.

Revival from shocked league of nightmarish war effects,
Still world falls far in pace to attain matching access.
Which has affected to various orders of social forte,
Creating draped hysteria of evil cast, in colossal pose.

It is high time, that revolution has
become need of hour,
Only revolution can redeem world from ill spelt power.
However, school of thought for initiation of revolution,
More competently has to be set by theorized citation.

Now it's conscious revolution, fits to matched solution
Social revolution, intellectual revolution, peace revolution,
Economic revolution, cultural revolution etc. in lacy so on
Revolutions only can spell fit match for changes of dawn

In the event, all paces should be of revolutionary cadre
'We are Revolution', the slogan should be of loudest blare
By chanting craze, the march should be led to goal in set
Surely, by revolutionary spirit all disorders should be dealt.

Conscious revolution is corner stone for renewal whole
That churning out of reformed era thus can be an accord
If by matched conscience efforts, issues are scored
That desired outcome, surely will distinctly spell heady forge.

The Renaissance within . . .
Orbindu Ganga

The known had smelled deep
Into our conscience, stalled,
The flow from the thoughts
Have wriggled for ages, gnawed,
Avarice had surged infinitely into
The veins deeply thawed, perplexed,
Deeply rooted within the layers
For a period of time, mime to remain,
Seeing the contusion laid within the
Commune, dare a word was gushing.

Inception form drizzled the smile
With a thought, raising eyebrows,
Yestreen thoughts were routed
In the shadows, to be dusted forever,
The conscience lifted the conscious
To uproot the glean, to cleave the traces,
Words gathered momentum to synergize
The nigh ones, to share the smiles,
Little fingers held the placards with their
Guardians, to make others rinse in rain.

The forms need time to listen
To the desolated, to know the hardships,
The vulnerable to be given support for
Their livelihood to thrive, to think beyond,
Care to be volleyed among the youth to follow
It piously, leading the way for the younger ones,
Kindness to be wafted with the drops squirted
From childhood, to ameliorate the pauses,
Respect to be gardened in the hearts
Melting for the impecunious, to become a being.

Thawed the lifeline for many preoccupied
Flowing gutters, never to have realized,
The conscious renaissance laid the impetus
To see the sea change, to see the waves in the sea.

The Speech of a Common Crow
Rehanul Hoque

Everyone gets moved by beauty
I'm dirty, black and ugly
But my ugliness turned to be a boon although
Nobody longs for me, nobody cares
Nobody sings paean in honor of an ugly bird
The reason everyone disregards ugliness-
Helped me to remain free from slugfest with others
In the question of superiority!
Never do I aspire to be a human – the great creature,
Rather moving unfettered to every nook and cranny
Of the planet, from one open landscape to another,
From treeless tundra to rocky cliff, riverbank,
Deserts, scrubby woodland and where not-
I'm at ease.

I have no country or confines of race and color
Nor any 'Ism' that superior beings boast of,
My feelings as a tiny creature rendered me the liberty
To drink life to the lees!
Born in a Spanish laboratory testifying to
Human technological feat, I'm linked with mankind
Find interest on human affairs
I'm a common crow, a nasty bird
You find within your arm's throw.

I'm happy that life gave me without stint
I've seen kingdoms and empires,
Civilization and elite, peasants and bourgeois
I reminisce about travelling along Kolyma road
Long ago, I saw civilization built over
Uranium and gold, how flesh was used as mortar and
Bones as stones- covered with asphalt!
I remember a small kid standing on the way
Looking for its dad among living dead,
A wife that awaited a dear face the entire life
Besides living with someone else, attending household chores;
A mother dazed by the news her son is no more
Looked blank, she lost her speech for good.

W.A.R. ~ *We Are Revolution*

I thought in my mind this is the path
That saw millions of the superior race,
Driven in droves to camps to extract riches
With a dream to get handsome salary and decent life,
Their dreams were never fulfilled
Their stories became history
 None was charged with murder, in contrary,
'Murder' was coined to introduce a crow family
Yet we don't care since we didn't commit anything heinous.
We stand beside ourselves in danger, uphold fellow-feeling
Not by mourning the dead, but by chasing predators in a manner
You call as 'mobbing', although it is our helplessness
In the face of existential crisis.

I never read history but among superior beings
I saw a partition, done with the stroke of pencil
Consequently, a great mass migration and ghost trains
Commuting between stations of two countries-
Carrying severed breasts, amputated limbs and organs
I'm the witness how a Sikh girl was carried on shoulder,
Taken behind a bush, laid down on ground-
The hero ready to trump her right away
Found a heap of cold flesh- yet he performed well!
Human beings call such an act as Necrophilism
The course offers opportunity to learn its symptoms,
Curing methods and free practical classes
At midnight hours.

I never attended a University nor do anyone of us
We learn whatever we see-
Learn to identify every individual, place and thing
This is the gift we're endowed with, never try to exploit
Dead rattlesnakes with their sensors do it minutely
Humans imitated the technique, produced biochips,
Identifying cameras and auto surveillance system-
No doubt, an advancement to take pride in!
But it brought devastation to the life of a young girl
Her nude photos became viral on Facebook, Twitter and social media
Everyone relished her nude beauty, rotund breasts
And fleshy butt- she had to pay with her life.

Poets for Humanity

I build my house using twig, twine and bark
Which bear no record anytime, anywhere, any member
Of my family had to lose eyesight in building a nest!

But in a trip to Taj Mahal, to my wit's end, I saw
Thousands of carvers becoming blind while erecting
A monument of love over a dead body.

In an urge for relaxation, standing on anthill
I look for anting- which allows me to ward off parasites
Thus, I revel in the sweetness of life.
Humans rush in the pub, get drunk
Commit sex at night, everything is finished.
If winning an unknown beauty becomes so easy
In a society, isn't love but nine days' wonder there!

I'm a dirty, black and ugly bird
Despite my cawing being shrilling and cacophonous to you
You may have trust on me- my words are never gimmick
I know not betrayal, fraudulence and duplicity
But I have seen how skillfully the con artists perform on stage
Taking oath under Oath Act, 1929.

Seeing all these I have decided, given chance of a rebirth
And choices between life of a celebrity and an ugly crow
I would opt for the latter for a single day instead of
Hundreds of years of a glorious biped.

Now
Sandra Mooney-Ellerbeck

Embrace
meadows where dragonflies glide,
bees, butterflies and unity thrives—
Embrace
evergreens where eagles rise,
solidary seeds spread below—
Embrace
birch, aspen, willow; all of earth's lungs—
Embrace
sacred spaces of consciousness, void
of smog and neon—
Embrace
the wild, the planted, transplanted,
every mountain, land/sky scape,
every stream, river and sea—
Embrace
even rain collected in barrels—
Embrace
water as if it is breath flow—
harbor an ark of love
where diverse blessings grow—
Embrace
solution in balance in evolution,
where hope is to risk and to risk
is to live—
Embrace
nature's language before the dialogue
is forgotten—
before destruction numbs sensibility,
before virtual reality is all
that is known of nature
and humanity's embrace—
Embrace
the pulse of passion
to breathe—
Embrace
now.

We Are the Revolution
Nassira Nezzar

When your world grows dark
and your soul feels heavy
Drowning in oppression, discrimination or in a failure
No amount of guilt can change the past
No amount of anxiety can change the future
Rise up from your ashes
By climbing the mountains of courage
Prepare yourself for the worse by will and willingness
Life is unpredictable and you're the only responsible for your happiness
You should never forget we're the revolution
Change is inevitable to our evolution
We should never let the hands of our dreams shake deception
We should defeat the internal enemy of fear and hesitation
When we learn to control and direct our minds
We can direct our internal voices to work for us
Rather than against us
If we want to live our dreams in reality
We have to fight for them daily

Growingly, We Are Revolution
C. S. P. Shrivastava

We say
We are not at war
We are though
In a lo
The Social
Consciousness
The ego underlying
Inviting n resulting
In devastation n
Annihilation –
Mass or partial –
All ago
Of cultural values
Inherited or passed onto
Are but at stake
The very basis of
Our being – the funding stone
Of our glories –
Past preserved
Are all gone –
In a go –
We need to be at war
Against the notions
Concepts and all the seeds sown –
For a concept healing
Being at Revolution
Is a change –
We need n solicit
As a free seeker now.

The Revolution of Hearts: For a Harmonious Humanity
Lovelyn P. Eyo

Our world so ill
It seeks a-healing
The bond of unity severed into pieces
Gloom and doom left on faces
Faces of war peeping around places

Choking smiles choking speech
Rashes of evil hearts itch

Truth upended
Morality trampled, not ended
Justice blinded
Injustice founded
For huge money traded

Sacrificing females
On the altar of slavery and inequality
Fostering oneness? A fail

Images of richness frown at the poor
They treat as outcast slammed doors
Clinching fist of selfishness
Rather than extending open hands of kindness
For humankind is truly about showing kindness
One hand in another
Uplifting one another

We all are of red blood
Warm veins packed human style
Why hate innocent colours of life
Letting veins flow in flood
Of evil bile

W.A.R. ~ We Are Revolution

Humanity tilted
Humankind wilted
With promoting misdeeds
Unity ought we breed

Humanity means –
Humans in unity
Why not value its integrity
As the earth revolves
Oneness round the sun
Our hearts must revolve
Under the sun
Birthing seasons of peace and love for all

"Transforming hearts" –
Is transforming and healing humanity
Let's make this heart's revolution
Our true resolution

Let's stop the discrimination
Stop the oppression
Stop the injustice
Let's stop fighting peace!

Peace thou not bid adieu
But it be what we adore
Stopping every drumbeats
Of inhumanity and disunity
But resounding our heartbeats
With the rhythm of compassion love and peace

Let's be this home
To make the world a harmonious home

Do Not Give Up
Elvirawati Pasila

Time passed worryingly
Raises a question in my mind
Who knows when the seasons changing
This pandemic will end soon, hopefully

Do not give up, we are struggling together
Learn to weave hope in the digital era
Rifles are not our mainstay
But at our fingertips the liberating of stupidity

We must be able to make friends with technology
On the internet network reach all dreams
There was no distance between us
Teachers and students keep meeting
Sharing knowledge,
Make achievements
And the world knows . . .
We are still here and won't give up.

A Voice to the Quest
Priya Unnikrishnan

Comrades,
Which way to the street of
Revolutionary warm blankets?
Between heaven and earth
The city changed to drought
The lakes defeated the deserts
In a single bet.
Colorless Spring of Withered
Flowers proclaiming
The Fall of bare twigs.
Foreseeing the wintry,
It can be toxic to the blood
Brain and soil.
Comrades,
Which way to the street of
Revolutionary warm blankets?
To prevent the disguised sleep
And to not sleep.

can we
Arti Rai

can we ask these snooty missiles
and weapons of mass destruction
to put their lofty heads down and
rest in peace forever with the hope of
no second coming in this world

can we ask these giant tanks
loaded with venomous artilleries
which flare hatred and reek of violence
over human's earth of dreams

can we can we all for the
sake of our children stand
as nation in solidarity to burry
our armories under the grave

can we make a ring of harmony
joining hands bereft of smells
of religion and painful boundaries
say if we can do this act so humanly

and let this world respire some
peace some hope when all the world
is a suffering house wherein folks
have refuged under spiky canopy

of illness death and agony
can we lend ahead a helping hand
i plea to the citizens all over the globe

tell if we can undo all the
guilty past and breed a new breeze
without smoke of treachery

tell if we can ask our lame vanity
to die at once and level our clashes

my tender heart demands
an absolute makeover

W.A.R. ~ We Are Revolution

Revolutionize Consciously from Within
Anamika Bhattacharya

Mother Earth bellowed her trumpet
Hollering drums, blowing her wrathful conch,
Taking in the human race within its storming fury
Gulping down millions of souls at a time
Whether it is in the guise of pandemic
Or wildfire or blasts or incessant rains
Followed by floods,
The ire of our beloved beholder
Looks to be at Her wit's end,
Nay . . . this is no sudden rigour
Or an abrupt erupting of fury
But, a long patient waiting
A consciously planned revolution
A way of nature's musing,
Nature's reverie and patient bearing
Of all the selfish, non-compromising
Unpardonable acts by mankind,
After aeons of pain bearing
Nature has unleashed its patient forbearing
And is screaming, howling to humans
No More! The Day of Judgment is here.

A patient love effulging compassionate mother
Has at last broken her silence
And screaming a huge war cry,
A conscious and planned way of revolting
And saying- No more!
No Mother henceforth would tolerate
The heinous misdeeds of her child,
It's time for a payback
To prepare your ledgers, you calculative Shylocks,
Time to pay back every cent you owe is now
With death dancing a cosmic dance
On the heads of every living human
Unless you realize why you are –

Living . . .
Breathing . . .
Scintillating and pulsating in this glorious bounty
You will but perish like many already gone.

Time for humanity to wake up and ponder
Why 2020 is aptly the revolution?
From a silent pain enduring Mother Nature
Unless you wish to live a dead, unrealized
Non-emancipated, effervescent life
The possibilities galore that nature
Would not provide you with such opportunity,
It is time for you to gear up
To a consciously planned revolution from within
To change yourself and mold according
As nature's norms act,
Come O humanity and the earthly souls
Bathe in the pure conscious
Evolve from within as responsible earthlings
Breathe in the conscious revolution to change thyself,
As one who cares and nurtures
The beauty that Mother Nature brings forth blessings
Else in a moment's lapse
Is engulfed, taken into the great expanse
Return from where an impossible possibility
Unless the Supreme Identity
So wishes the being to be!!!

Because of Love
S. Pathmanathan ('Sopa')

The child was crying endlessly
He won't take his food
He brushed aside overtures by his parents
Exhausted, he fell asleep.
The only child of a Saudi millionaire
heir to numerous companies
he was nursed
by a Sri Lankan house maid

She was everything to him
She used to feed him, wash him
change his linen
play with him
The boy used to sleep with her
not with his mother!

Therein lay the hitch
The maid had gone on leave
to meet her family in Sri Lanka
From the moment she left
the boy refused to take his meals
He cried, cried and cried
till his throat became hoarse

His parents thought
he would wake up hungry
and eat something.
That was not to be
The child was rushed to the hospital
He was put on a drip
No improvement
The doctors said 'Fetch the maid!'
The millionaire sent frantic messages
but the maid won't relent!
Her husband was sick

Poets for Humanity

He needed medical attention
The master offered to fly her husband
And her children to Saudi Arabia

Things moved quickly
The maid's family arrived in two days
She was rushed to the hospital
Seeing the boy's state she wailed in Tamil!
"Aadil, my darling Aadil", she wept
The boy's toe stirred
The doctors signaled
The maid continued : "Aadil, Aadil my boy!"
Slowly he came to himself
Freed himself from the life-supporting system
He hugged the maid
smothered her with kisses!
The maid's husband was treated
In the same hospital
Her children are now attending
an International School in Saudi Arabia

In a world
where men kill each other
in the name of
color or creed
land or language
Where camps keep teeming with refugees
an illiterate woman
has a message for the warmongers
LOVE
transcending borders and barriers!

The Gifts a Breeze Carries
Anju Kishore

Why do you smell of blood, you ask me?
Follow me as I blow over lands you haven't seen.
Let me show you lives that straddle pain and death
In worlds where justice is on its last breath.

You shall blow with me across a child's window
To watch him play the games you know.
But his childhood is not the blessing you call yours.
He plays dodge with bullets in his bombed corridors.

Let us slip together through hospital dorms
That have let in bleeding, entire towns.
Rushed in are grocers and teachers, soldiers and more.
Rolled out is death or something close.

Glorified is life as a gift in your world.
Here horrors are unleashed as lives unfurl.
Wars leave children orphaned and maimed
Men dead and women shamed.

What gifts can I bring you other than the sense
Of loss and utter hopelessness?
Send me back if you can to those unhappy places
With gifts of peace and love's fragrances.

Send me back if you can with poetry
For bleeding in wars of words is humanity.
Futile they claim is the mind's wanderlust
Its paeans to beauty, roses and stardust.

Lost are their paths, buried their signs in an eternal night
Remind them of the stars, their guiding light.
Send them the whispers of the endless seas
So they unite with their souls that run as deep.

Poets for Humanity

Pin on to my wings, the music of your mystic lines
And bid me bear the universe on my flight.
Let me descend softly on their ravaged dawns
And hand them a sunray to script their songs.

So the flowers smell no more of orphaned homes
And soot need be wiped by the moon no more
Let me kiss the hearts of those with bloodthirsty plans
Send me back if you can, to those lands.

Do Not Be Suspicious
Tara Noesantara

Light up all the lanterns of the universe so that this earth becomes hell . . .
Let the flames of fighting do not you put out
The red ants lined up strong
Call and be your ally
Get rid of deep dreams
Battalion troops dare to die . . .
Get rid of the ghosts of the land that mess up the laws
Free our house from the undermining of iron fist
Free our home from fools
Wild trash scattered
Which has ruined culture
Stop everything
With the hope of guarding each other and being alert
Because the neighbors are suspicious of each other . . .
Stop meaningless propaganda
Each human being has power . . .

The Rest of Heritage
Yanz Haryo Darmista

What else remains of the splendor of the past

Except for the wounds and sorrows of the present

From the upheaval that never goes out never goes away . . .

I'm just a lump of meat with no definite direction

Where should I step if the earth is full of wounds

My moi only left a small nature no more than a throw of footsteps

A crutch that has become brittle . . .

Stepping over the bustle of the city

Take care of . . . take care of this little inheritance

So that everyone can enjoy it too

Full of memories from time to time

From a goal full of collision . . .

An Intellectual Crusade
Dr. Thirupurasundari C. J.

Gun fires, sunken hearts,
Violence in memory, life-time ineffaceable scars,
Martyrs in graveyard,
Heartbreaking turbulences of kith and kin,
Huge funded wars,
Tremendous budgetary pressures,
Infrastructure, social order, education hampered,
Peace and health gone for a toss
Economic fabric of the nation, devastated,
Productivity deteriorated,
Misplaced people, damaged property, cultural drifts,
Domestic violence too has a share-miserable though,
Vulnerable become the female sex,
Human race psychologically affected,
Horrific casualties,
Social unrest everywhere!
War fades in few months,
After-effects last for decades,
It spans across generations,
Ponder on it! Love our planet.

Duty of mankind, to uphold justice,
Restructure the economy,
Impregnate growth, developmental goals.

Pain may nourish courage, if war is in pursuit of freedom,
Loaded with obstacles, is the journey to freedom,
Intellectual and practical mind, the dire need,
May our broken hearts refuel us!
Overhauling our mental abilities,
Let scars make people more munificent.

As regiments raise, equip and train troops,
Our borders be secured and safe,
Mitigate global tensions,
Develop amicable ties with neighbours,

Poets for Humanity

Promote stress- free co-existence,
Dissuade weapon sales,
Prohibit beguile of nuclear ammunitions.

Need of the hour,
Disarmament, diplomacy, human security,
Conciliation, mediation and technology transfer,
Revolutionize health sectors,
May our students represent global citizens!
Help create a self-reliant nation.

Let media take a sensible role,
Debating real issues,
Spreading constructive conversations,
Not demoralizing our own soldiers,
Ought to remember,
Let their deaths, not go in vain.
Not essential are their exaggerations,
Lesser the noise, advocate peace and love,
Curb the stigmas.

Exhibiting hubris, clout, rebel is not the theme,
Negotiations and policy changes work,
Promote peace maneuvers,
Not to endure critical dearth of logic and kindness,
Express concern, respect cultural differences and beliefs,
Wage war against diseases, illiteracy, jealousy, hatred and privacy breaching.

Cherish co-existence and not co-destruction,
Peace starts with us,
Make an imperative difference by a holistic approach,
With all strength and integrity!

You Coming into My Life Was a Dream, You Left Me with Another Dream
Aditi Roy

I still remember the night you visited me.
It was a beautiful starry night
Your presence was sudden
My heart was beating fast
I hesitated in the beginning
I didn't how to start.
But you began and we spoke off those temporary promises.

It was a beautiful starry night
Your presence was sudden
My heart was beating fast
I remember you said you wanted to build a world
A world without fear
A world full of love
A world full of happiness
A world where we could be together

It was a beautiful starry night
Your presence was sudden
My heart was beating fast
You promised to be my muse
You promised that I would finally be writing my masterpiece

And then you slowly left
That night ended
Darkness descended

I stood by the window watched you bid me goodbye
I stood by the window and watched a new dawn come to my life.

I waited for you to come back again
I waited for you to be my muse yet again
But I only waited for you in an unkempt room
Still holding on to the pen you gave me

My eyes full of tears struck on the newspaper
I could finally create my masterpiece
I could finally live your dream

It was a beautiful starry night
Your presence was sudden
My heart was beating fast
But the dawn was not the same.
I seemed to have been reborn with a hope of a better tomorrow

Rat Race @ Lockdown
Kamar Sultana Sheik

What came as an immense 'pause',
Must be respected, as such;
The treadmill of the rat race
Was put on pause-mode . . .
A clear signal of an end,
And surely a new beginning . . .
Of taking it easy . . . and not 'racing' . . .
Yet, here we are, as incurable as ever!
We want certification after certification,
Upskilling, achievement and productivity . . .
The whole grinding machinery,
Of doing this, doing that,
Measuring lockdown productivity,
At a frenzied pace, matching bond-buying . . .
That adrenaline-powered mental machinery
Has simply forgotten how to rest!
Why, oh why do we not realize,
That it is 'you' and not 'yours',
That is going to count in the end . . .?
That after you're gone,
Those certificates on the walls
Will turn meaningless for you?
A Pandemic is in the air,
And we have still not realized
The meaning of 'breath' . . .
The rats and bats are surviving,
It is the human, caught up in the rat-race,
Refuses to become the 'being' of grace,
Remaining, a self-styled 'rat',
Living for the sake of a race!

Yet, and yet, now is when people could learn
The precious lessons of finding themselves,
Of grieving for others,
Their conversations with their shadows . . .

Poets for Humanity

The art of aloneness and its many healings.
So that people could find their way back to prayer
And Meditation and restful-ness..
And give up their dangerous heartlessness . . .
Creating a wise new world!

W.A.R. ~ *We Are Revolution*

Revolutionized
Gayle Howell, AKA Lady Silk

I used to be dedicated to the cause
But then the cause took hold of me
Broke me down into so many pieces
Till I couldn't justify my own being
Change is coming though
And it's coming on fast.
It feels as though I am being birthed
And rejoicing at the task
As we dance and sing song
I become aware and recognize at last
That I hold the revolution within
And she's uprising against the past

I am a revolution
Giving birth to a new nation within myself
I said; I am the revolution
And I stood tall during time itself
You see I am the revolution
That they say would never come
Hell, I am the revolution
After enslaving me, was done
Yet he thinks he holds the power over me
Trying to hold me up under lock-n-key
Not understanding nor seeing
The uprising woman within me

I shall act out of rebellion
And revolt against this authority
Just because he thinks he holds
The power over me
Holding my back up against the sea
Not understanding
Nor seeing the uprising within thee
You see, I am that revolution
And will no longer allow him to overpower me
I am the revolution
      I am the revolution!
            I*AM*THE*REVOLUTION

The Sound of Glowing Echoes
Kay Salady

Virulence sends its thunder
As turbulent waves come crashing
We quake . . . the earth trembles with us
Screaming out in pain
Giving birth to revolution
The night sky brings a cover of peace
As if to comfort the wounded
The moon conducts a symphony
Releasing candles lit with fervent prayer
She tilts her lilting head to hear
The sound of glowing echoes
That twinkle in the darkness
She stares down a starlit path
That leads us to forgiveness
In the silence of the suffering
Our many arrows fly
Piercing the hearts and minds
Of one another

W.A.R. ~ *We Are Revolution*

In a War Where No One Won,
In Our Love Won . . . Always One
Nutan Sarawagi

Wasn't I always one with you
Why did you break me into two
Dividing me
within me and you
Happy I lived content in you
Then you took me away with you
Breaking me in parts that were me
Now you
Why did you do this
Why did you
In my love your love undo
Born we were in one home one
In our Motherland won
To break us into many
that no more knew
each other's blood in them they drew
For weren't we one
why this sudden spurt of hate
their ploy to play each other in a political game
caught in their bait
fall prey to their vested interests fight in their hate

In your venom to hate me in you
Why this me and you
Let's just be you
If it makes you happy
I am no more you / me
But me with you
I live in you
Let's once again meet in love
In our world once again bind in love
In our national anthem to once again sing in love
In a love that meets in luv

Poets for Humanity

All hate evaporates as we all become love
One love in which we all turn in love
To just love
To unite in this love
No more hurt each other
No more divide our love
just love

A Prisoner
Terri L. Johnson, AKA 'Poetry Johnson'

I met a child.
She knew only so much.
She asked who I was.
My name is not important.
She asked me if I had food.
I gave her what I could.
She pointed to my eyes.
Then to her own.
She said the same.
I nodded in agreement.
She was so young,
fragile and sweet.
Where was her parents.
How has she survived.
How did she eat.
I asked where her parents were.
She said they died.
It was just her.
She said,
they have been gone
for many moons now.
There is no one.
No one but her.
I took her in.
Gave her love,
food and shelter.
She became my daughter.
My sun.
My moon.
My everything.
I became her mother.
Her world became mine.
She thrived in love.
I nurtured her
Fed her my soul.
A prisoner of sorts
Was that of where she came.
Now free,
At least to grow in love once again.

The Human Race Needs an All-Out Revolution
Gobinda Biswas

Humans are the most developed creatures on Earth
But they have all the vices of the Pandora's Box,
So since time immemorial they have been trying
To build the Babel Tower on the bodies of weakers.

The struggle between Good and Evil continues still
Since Cain and Abel for Cain hated the good latter,
While Moses had to cross the turbulent Red Sea,
With followers because of envious Faraoh, the dictator.

From pre-historic times labour-classes are deprived
But the aristocrats enjoy all and despise them,
All the humans across the world are one race
But they're divided within and without, it's a shame.

They're divided as the Hindu, Muslim, and Christian
Along with Buddhist, Joroastrian, Jew and Sikh,
Even today horrible apartheid continues everywhere
As society is disintegrated as the Black and White.

Millions have been tortured and brutally slain
For venomous vapour of communalism and racism,
Renaissance and French Revolution cruelly failed
Now humans need an all-out emotional revolution.

W.A.R. ~ *We Are Revolution*

The Insanity of Humanity
Loretta L. Hardrick

It is by far obvious to some and utterly oblivious to others, the impact of the actions and reactions that do not add to but are devasting subtractions,
to all my sisters and my brothers.

I must admit our afflictions are simply due to so many addictions. If not the addiction to drugs and alcohol, then it is social media, sports, sex, perversions
rather than nothing at all.

Perhaps my eyes are wide open to the hatred that is expressed, although I am a praying woman who strongly believes in God I am affected, nonetheless.

You see, I see from a different perspective, and through a different pair of eyes. I can listen to the conversations and see right past their lies.

What I see are selfish people, only concerned about being and staying number one. However, all good things must come to an end, but when will freedom and justice for all, ever really become?

Life is a precious commodity; we should not take it for granted nor treat it too lightly but even among our communities, we have digressed ever so mightily.

Innocent lives are snatched away from others in the twinkling of an eye, and there are no emotions of compassion if I should succumb to their fate and die.

What happened to the conscience, the consequences, and repercussions that should deter? Selfishness has superseded them all and humanity does what it prefers.

The problem is mathematics, too many subtractions, and not enough additions.

The problem is wanting the favor and grace of God but denying the power thereof, not adhering to His Word or giving it, its due attention.

The problem is there are too many withdrawals and not enough deposits. Offering these surface solutions knowing that they will never solve it.

The problem is there are too many get quick schemes, as well as "let me get you before you get me." This was not the intention, nor how it was meant to be.

Poets for Humanity

The problem is with the bitter ill regard of one toward another for various reasons. It is not only a slap to face of God but by all means, it is a form of treason.

The problem is with not standing up for righteousness, or anything innately related it is the attitude of self-righteousness which could easily be debated. It is willingly accepting not to do what is right. It is acceptable usage of bigotry as weapons and operating in deceit all through the night.

The insanity of humanity is wanting better without participating and becoming openly involved. And knowing what the solution should be but rather seeking a less challenging resolve.

Understand this and, yes, take heed. When humanity is accosted violently; red blood we all do bleed.

This seems to be a problem that is not going away, so we need to prepare to make changes or it will be our babies who will have to pay.

The insanity of humanity is this; expecting a positive result of love and caring when the virus of hatred, social, and economic injustices are spread daily.

If you think I am exaggerating; the magnitude of deaths weighs heavily.

If we genuinely desire change and transformation, God is the necessary means which can change the course of every nation.

If we truly expect a peaceful environment in which we can safely live, we must begin to follow the Word of God which tells us that we are to give and continue to give.

Give without expectation of restitution, give because He gave and allowed humanity a God-given resolution. The insanity of humanity is willing to sell out its soul for wealth, and to kill just to be killing to satisfy its sinful self.

If we continue to choose not to follow the Word of God to the letter, then do not by any means expect our living conditions to ever change or get any better.

Humanity wants what it wants, when it wants it and how it wants it but that is contrary to the Word of God. I pray I cry out, and there are still those who tend to rob.

The Kingdom suffers violence, just look around and see. Even the violent attempt to take, yes take it forcibly.

W.A.R. ~ *We Are Revolution*

If we as a people would be willing to let our lives mirror the image of Christ, changes would be imminent and real change would be our new way of life.

If the insanity of humanity could in itself surrender and conclude, that all these decades of misguided fear and hatred have hindered our progression by carelessly being sadistically rude.

Insanity is doing the same thing over and over yet expecting a different result. "Wake up," humanity it is nigh time we begin to seek God's help.

Against Ineffable Man
Krishna Prasai

I asked the gun, the gunpowder and fire,
"Are your heat, the burn and the sizzle
Enough to annihilate the human race?"
The gun started answering me:
It wanted to be a Buddha inside the closed barrel.

Gunpowder too had its grievances:
It wanted to repose, like a sage, in peace.
Fire too had an ambition beyond speculation:
It had the capacity, like the Himalayas
To bloom as the snow.
It had dreams, like that of a hill,
To put on new wings, and soar.

I wanted to know:
Why does the gun stand against the human race?
Why does a bullet target nothing but people?
To vanquish the gun, we now need a newer arm
Which can be vanquished
Only by the modest request of words.

The colour of war is
Far more gruesome that the burning charcoal!
No! We don't need such terrible ghastliness anymore.
I would rather add colours of lifelong faith
To my own dreams
And sleep carefree upon the mattress of peace
Against ineffable man.

W.A.R. ~ We Are Revolution

Jason's Poem
Jason Adams

think it's pretty neat.
It's not so safe to drive now cause your four wheel steed can't float
As the Mississippi River turns each town into a moat

Have you
Ever seen a simple breeze rip the roof off of a house?
As you have to hunker in a bunker with your dog, your kids, and spouse
And the little gust is roaring uprooting trees right from the ground
Not so little class 5 tornadoes don't make a pleasing sound

Global warming, we know it's not a Chinese hoax
Global warming, we can fix it with our votes
Turn your eyes from all the lies about renewable energy
Say good bye to corporate ties of the coal and oil industries
It will happen fast
if we just pass
the laws we know are right
Global warming we must all stand up and fight!

Have you
Ever seen an ocean ripple cause a wave that touched the sky?
impending tidal devastation makes you cry and you know why
The origami rolling tsunami that an earthquake sent along its way
Mother earths not so subtle warnings we ignore from day to day

Chorus

And the glaciers are all melting
The polar bears are dying
Volcanos are erupting
Most politicians are corrupting
As the oil lines are spilling
Flint Michigan's water is still killing
The temperature is rising
Global ignorance is mesmerizing

Chorus/out

I AM
"NUK-PUK-NUK"
"I am that I am"
Kedar Imani

I do not search for the "god" but rather find ways to allow the "god"
    to manifest through me . . .

I am imperfectly perfect; but I try to walk as if the whole world is watching . . .

I have never arrived on time . . . because I travel in time . . .

I am never late . . . I am always exactly where I'm supposed to be . . .

I am significantly insignificant; but without me the world would not have been incomplete

I am not a "human" being; but a "spiritual" being having a human experience

The vessel body that encompasses I am, is only my ship to navigate
    through this journey we call "life" . . .

To some I may appear knowledgeable; but all I really "know", is how little I really "know"

Sometimes I look but don't see . . . Sometimes I listen but don't hear

I am not just a drop in the ocean . . . I am the entire ocean in a drop

I walk with the "ancestors" . . . We are one!

"Special" I am not; but I am a "minute" part of the "All"!

I am that I am!

convoluted
hülya n. yılmaz

sitting still,
contemplating;
body, numbed,
knowing that neither a taser
nor a bullet touched it . . .
yet
feeling safe in the color of my skin
no one has despised or violated
any aspect of my external humanness . . .
yet

sitting still,
contemplating;
spirit, in grave despair,
crying me the longest river on Earth
the at-my-face pain and suffering
of my co-human beings
have eras ego been the writing on the wall for me –
a succinct display of one of the ugliest barbaric timelines,
of a collective guilt- and shame-canvas,
cloaked in a hooded "patriotic" cape
of the palest hue of white
a sight, i no longer can bear

sitting still,
contemplating;
mind, convoluted,
incapable of making any sense of it all –
all that which is taking place
again and again
and then . . .
once again

as i sit still,
mind, body and spirit
immersed in convolutions,

Poets for Humanity

my decades-long readings
come back to haunt me repeatedly;
for, those supposedly learn-ed
and often-regurgitated pages
cannot even begin to compare
to anything that has been unfolding
right before my eyes in this century,
as long as i have lived consciously
for a considerably extended period of time, that is,
and not just once, twice, thrice . . .
but again, again and again

what continues to dominate
the stance of the willfully ignorant –
ordinary people as well as the powers that be?
an age-old prejudice,
words of unconditional condemnation,
extremely negative stereotypes,
blatant injustice in the name of justice,
self-justifying acts of discrimination,
self-justifying acts of selective violence,
a wholehearted condoning of brutal murders
that are being committed against each soul
who happens to not share
my skin's particular hue

on and on, i ponder the events that transpire here and now
in the hope that a poem will eventually emerge
from the innermost turmoil
which each of my living cells senses to the core
having become a second skin,
my anguish weighs heavily on me,
it tears up and cries me the longest river on Earth
while my petite, fragile external frame
is faced with the onus of climbing a mountain
so massive that nothing which had prepared my self
mentally, psychologically, emotionally,
and spiritually in many a period of time before
comes even close to sufficing to serve
as a source of comfort for me anymore

W.A.R. ~ *We Are Revolution*

i then remember a calming fact,
namely that there is also a most powerful side of me:
an all-empowering monozygotic pregnancy!
it doesn't take me long at all to realize
that only the true "i" in me can carry my twins full-term
as can you through the "i" in you!
once born, our twins, Aequitas and Justitia
will begin their peaceful reign of goodness and truth
whatever is needed for an all-inclusive humanity,
they will instill in the hearts and minds of our youth

i am not the one to judge
if a poem has, indeed, materialized from my words
as for their impact – if any – it will remain unknown
but of one outcome i am absolutely sure:
i no longer feel any despair;
for, that self-defeating state of existence
is replaced by a boldly deep resolve
in which i unhesitatingly let myself dissolve
it is there where Ludwig Uhland's painless joy
cradles me inside a kissing breeze:

"Oh fresh scent, oh new sound!
Now, poor heart, fear not!
Now everything, everything must change."

convoluted?
no more!

This poem represents but one of the dynamics within humanity that is screaming for a need of change . . . bias, bigotry, racism.

What If I Were to Tell You . . .
William S. Peters, Sr.

The best thing since chocolate cake,
For there is not any
Angel Food cake left,
It has all been consumed
By the greed of the illusion

Soldier, soldier,
What if I were to tell you
That the wars you fight,
And the 'country'
You are willing to kill for
Cares not a damn thing
About you and your loved ones

What if I were to tell you,
That your efforts,
Your sacrificed lives
Enrich those
Who profit from conflict,
And prosper greatly
When you die

Yes, there is a reason!!!

How many bullets and bombs
Did you use today?
How many people
Did you kill today,
Or yesterday,
While visiting
Their country . . .
Did you know them?
Any of them?
What was your death-beef
With them,

W.A.R. ~ *We Are Revolution*

Their families,
Their villages and towns,
Or their way of life?

Did you know
That they are human too?

Politics,
Resources,
Weapons manufacturers
And
Arms sales
Are all good motivations
For you to die today,
'Them' to die today,
And tomorrow too!

Patriotism,
Democracy?
Damn, we have problems here,
Right here at 'Home'
We have yet to resolve

Mass murderers,
Terrorist,
State sanctioned
Death and brutality

Will we,
Any of us,
Ever be absolved
Of our sins?
I doubt it!
. . .
Sodom and Gomorrah
Live on,
Cloaked in another filthy deceptive
Cloth

Poets for Humanity

Hate,
Unjustified Hate,
Is the 'Chic' thingee
Of these days,
Better rush on down
To Wal Mart
Or Piggly Wiggly
And get yourself a box of Bigotry . . .

Better yet,
Buy a case

And feed it to your children,
NOW,
While they can still
Be poisoned,
In a delusional 'Self-Righteous' manner

I am tired,
How about you?

Time for change yet?

Humanity,
We have been wearing
These soiled diapers
For far too long,
To the point
That we have become accustomed
To the stench . . .

Why, there are many
Who live to relish
The funk
Of their own breath,
And that of others
Who spew that

W.A.R. ~ *We Are Revolution*

Shit laden vitriol
That they believe
Their Jesus, Mohammad,
Krishna and Buddha
Would love . . .

Fucking hypocrites!!!!!

What if I told you
That none of you are going to
Hell . . . why,
Because you are living in it
At this very moment,
And it is going to get
Much hotter

What if I were to tell you . . .
Fuck You!!!!

I have a better idea . . .
'Love thy neighbor'

Poets for Humanity

W. A. R.

we are revolution

Essays,

Critiques

and

Creative Prose

Essays, Critiques and Creative Prose

In this section, you will have the opportunity to visit upon the voices of a diverse group of thinkers. Some voices may appear to be imposing while others are considerable and congruous to your present way of thinking. The purpose of *W. A. R., We Are Revolution* is to potentially expand our awareness of some of the nuances that affect humanity in profound ways. We, Inner Child Press International, do not take a position of endorsing any of the views, philosophies or theosophies of any of the contributors. Our perspective of including this section was to offer to you a diversity that represents a few factions of the human genome. In being true to our motto, 'building bridges of cultural understanding', our hope is to stimulate or create additional thought and dialogue that bring us closer to the conceptualization and acceptance of this said diversity. This opportunity, we feel, is the initiative and catalyst to change when we consider the contemplations, examinations and perspectives of others.

Thank you.

Inner Child Press International
'building bridges of cultural understanding'

> SCHÜLER
> Doch ein Begriff muß bei dem Worte sein
> MEPHISTOPHELES
> Schon gut! Nur muss man sich nicht allzu ängstlich quälen;
> Denn eben wo Begriffe fehlen
> Da stellt ein Wort zur rechten Zeit sich ein
>
> Goethe, *Faust I*, Studierzimmer

Wanderer
Gino Leineweber

Zwei Wanderer wandern umher. Manches Mal gehen sie gemeinsam. Manches Mal nicht. Sie können sowohl 'Grumpy Old Men' sein, oder Rivalen, oder zwei Gefährten, die sich entweder seit langer Zeit schätzen oder ablehnen. Es ist nicht einfach zu beschreiben, was es ist, aber sie vermitteln den Eindruck, irgendwie miteinander verbunden zu sein.

Wir folgen ihnen auf ihrem Weg die dreihundertfünfzig Stufen hinab von der winzigen byzantinischen Tsambika Kloster Kathedrale, die, mit einem atemberaubenden Ausblick über die Ägäis, auf einem ungefähr dreihundert Meter hohen Hügel steht. Sie sind auf ihrem Weg von Lindos nach Rhodos City. Beim Hinuntergehen sprechen sie über die Energie der kleinen Kapelle. Der Legende nach werden alle Frauen, die Probleme mit der Empfängnis haben, mit Kindern gesegnet, wenn sie die vielen Stufen hinaufgestiegen sind und zur Jungfrau Maria gebetet haben.

Sie sprechen ruhig miteinander, was darauf hindeutet, dass ihre Meinungen bezüglich des Themas nicht kontrovers sind. Der Wanderer, der mehr von seinem Herzen geleitet wird, glaubt, dass niemand genau wissen kann, welche Art von Energie uns tatsächlich umgibt, und dass es womöglich eine gäbe, die Einfluss auf körperliche Veränderungen haben könnte und womöglich mit einem bestimmten Gebet ausgelöst werden kann. Der andere indes, der von seinem Verstand geleitet ist, sagt, dass er denke, dass es nur einen Weg der Empfängnis gebe und dieser kein Gebet sei.

Beide wollen offensichtlich die Begleitung des anderen bei dieser Wanderung, aber man kann nie wissen. Es könnte schnell zu Differenzen kommen, worauf sie dann lieber ihrer eigenen Wege gehen und manchmal beschimpfen und verfluchen sie sich gar zum Abschied.

Rhodos hat sie, mit den vielfältigen Naturschönheiten, der hügeligen Landschaft, den lieblichen Pinien und Zypressenwäldern, Weinbergen und teilweise beeindruckend alten Olivenbäumen, in einen entspannten Zustand versetzt, in dem sie gelassen ihre Gedanken austauschen. Die Attraktivität der Insel wird durch deren alte Gemäuer verstärkt, wie die beiden Wanderer beobachten konnten, als sie auf ihrer Tour an der sogenannten Villa Mussolini vorbeikamen. Sie war für den früheren italienischen Diktator gedacht, falls er sich

nach dem erwarteten Sieg im Krieg in Griechenland aufhalten wollte Aber, wie jeder weiß, gab es keinen Sieg. Er hat niemals sein Haupt in dieser Region zur Ruhe betten können. Ihm blieb dieses hügelige Landschaftskunstwerk mit dem auserlesenen Ausblick über grüne Täler bis hinab zur Ägäis verborgen. Die Villa ist verkommt mit der Zeit. Doch die demolierten Fenster, Türen und Dächer, die hellen Wände mit dem bunten Graffiti auf blätterndem blau-gelben Grund erscheinen als ein ästhetisches Baukunstwerk. Genau wie die Ruinen der historischen Burgen und Festungen. Obwohl der Einfluss des Tourismus nicht ignoriert werden kann, charakterisiert sich die Insel durch ihr geschichtliches Vermächtnis. Nicht allein dem der Gebäude, sondern auch der Gastfreundschaft ihrer Bewohner, wie die Wanderer an einem sonnigen Nachmittag erleben durften. Nachdem sie einen Bergkamm mit unzähligen Höhlen unter den Gipfeln, den „Höhlen von St. George" überquert hatten, setzen sie sich für ein Erfrischungsgetränk in eine Taverne, die neben einer kleinen Kapelle liegt. Die Wirtsleute, ein Ehepaar mit einer kleinen Tochter, reichten zu den bestellten Getränken einen kleinen Imbiss auf Kosten des Hauses.

In Rhodos City, saßen sie an einem Vormittag auf einer Bank auf dem Bürgersteig gegenüber der Taverne Ateya. Sie ist nach ihrem Besitzer, einem Ägypter, benannt, der ihnen am Abend zuvor frische Garnelen serviert hatte, die er direkt vor seinem Laden zubereitete. Besser gesagt, der Grill stand direkt vor ihnen auf der Straße, mit einem beeindruckenden Sonnenuntergang am Horizont dahinter.

Einer der Wanderer zeigte nun auf eine Skulptur, die sich in der Mitte eines Kreisverkehrs zu ihrer Linken befindet und sagte:

„Weißt du wer das ist?"

„Natürlich weiß ich das. Diagoras. Er war einer der Helden von Rhodos."

„Ja," erwiderte der andere, „das hier ist eine richtig Heldeninsel", und sie begannen, sich darüber zu unterhalten.

Zuerst ist da natürlich der legendenumwobene Held, der dem großen Gott von Rhodos, Helios, geweiht war, der Koloss von Rhodos zu nennen. Er war und ist der bekannteste. Tatsächlich basiert seine Berühmtheit auf der früheren Statue, die als eines der Sieben Weltwunder angesehen wurde.

„Lass uns über die richtigen Helden sprechen, die Rhodos hervorgebracht hat, wie Leonidas von Rhodos, der berühmteste Olympiateilnehmer der Antike, der in vier aufeinanderfolgenden Olympischen Spielen[1] die Goldmedaillen auf drei unterschiedlichen Rennstrecken gewann."

„Ja," sein Begleiter lächelt, „man kann kaum glauben, dass dieser antike Rekord erst in 2016 von dem Amerikaner *Michael Phelps* gebrochen wurde. Über 2.000 Jahre später." Er schüttelt ungläubig den Kopf und fügte hinzu: „Leonidas ist wohl auch in dem Stadion in der antiken Akropolis von Rhodos City gelaufen, wo wir gestern auf unserem Weg eine Rast eingelegt haben."

„Natürlich ist er dort gelaufen. Und als wir uns dort auf den Stufen ausruhten, habe ich mir ihn ein wenig vorgestellt. Ein Rennen von einer Runde, die, wie du weißt, *stadion* genannt wurde und seinerzeit als Königsdisziplin der Olympischen Spiele galt. Vor meinem geistigen Auge startete Leonidas inmitten einer Gruppe von fast zwanzig anderen Läufern, und, der damaligen Sitte entsprechend, waren sie splitterfasernackt. Unser Held kam am schnellsten weg und lag die ganze Zeit in Führung. Die Kampfrichter hatten keine Mühe, ihn als Sieger zu küren, woraufhin er auf den Schultern einer begeisternden Menge unter triumphalen Ovationen herumgetragen wurde."

„Sehr schönes Bild," kam die Antwort, „einige Jahrhunderte weiter zurück hättest du mit deinem geistigen Auge Diagoras boxen sehen können. Höchstwahrscheinlich inmitten tausender aufgeregter Zuschauer, die ihm begeistert zujubelten. Er war auch ein *periodonikis*, ein Seriensieger, und hat, außer in Rhodos in einer ganzen Reihe anderer lokaler Wettbewerbe gewonnen, in Athen, Theben, Argos, Megara, Aegina. Am wichtigsten aber: er hat alle griechischen Spiele gewonnen – die Olympischen, die Pythianischen, sogar vier Mal die Isthmianischen und zweimal die Nemeanischen Spiele. Aber er war nicht nur berühmt wegen seiner eigene Siege, sondern auch wegen der vieler seiner Familienmitglieder." Der Wanderer wies erneut auf den Kreisverkehr: „Die Skulptur zeigt ihn im Jahre 448 vor Christus und Diagoras war da schon ein alter Mann. Zwei seiner Söhne, die am selben Tag Olympiasieger geworden waren . . ."

„. . . Ja, ich weiß – während sie von der Masse begeistert gefeiert wurden, hoben sie ihren Vater auf die Schultern, und das zeigt die Statue hier. Der Legende nach rief ein Spartaner aus der Menge: ‚Jetzt kannst du sterben, Diagoras, denn ein Gott wirst du nicht werden!' Gemeint war damit, Diagoras habe das höchste Glück eines Sterblichen auf Erden erreicht. Tatsächlich soll er an dem Tag im Applaus der Menge gestorben sein.

„Du weißt das natürlich. Aber weißt du auch, sein Ruhm wurde vom antiken Dichter *Pindar* gefeiert?"[2]

„Gewiss, weiß ich das. Und weil wir gerade von Dichtern sprechen, können wir auch sie

---

[1] 164-152 v. Chr.
[2] Pindar von Theben (Olympian Odes VII)

in unsere Heldenliste von Rhodos einordnen. Ich denke da an *Timocreon*."[3]

Beide lachten, denn dieser Poet war kaum als ein Gigant für sein poetisches Werk anzusehen, das ohnehin nur in Fragmenten überliefert ist. Er war berühmt für seine ausschweifenden Verse und Trinkgelage und betrachtete sich selbst als Athlet und Genießer.

„Erinnere dich, was am Hof des Königs von Persien geschah. Er hatte soviel gegessen, dass der König auf ihn zutrat und fragte, was er mit dieser Völlerei bezwecken wolle. Timocreon antwortete, er wolle sich in Form bringen für die unzähligen Perser, die er im Kampf zu besiegen gedachte, was er am nächsten Tag tatsächlich tat. Nachdem er alle Gegner geschlagen hatte, boxte er in die Lüfte, nur um zu zeigen, über wie viel Kampfkraft er noch für jeden verfügte, der es wagen sollte, es mit ihm aufzunehmen".[4]

„Woher weißt du das denn?"

„Vom alten griechischen Rhetoriker Athenaeus von Naukratios. Rhetorik bringt mich im Übrigen zu einer anderen historischen Figur, die ich als Held von Rhodos nennen möchte: *Aeschines*."

„Das ist nicht dein Ernst. Der stammte doch gar nicht aus Rhodos, sondern aus Athen.[5]"

„Das ist richtig. Dennoch. Hier in Rhodos hat er seine berühmte Rhetorikschule eröffnet. Du kannst dir auch ihn gut vor deinem geistigen Auge in der Akropolis vorstellen. Du musst nur vom Stadion aus ein wenig nach Nordwesten gehen, um das Odeon zu finden, wo er seine Vorträge vor ungefähr achthundert Zuhörern gehalten haben mag."

„Leider," entgegnete der andere düster, „kann ich das nicht, weil von dem kleinen Marmortheater nichts mehr übrig ist. Aber, entscheidender ist, dass ich deinen Rhetoriker nicht als Helden bezeichnen würde."

„Das ist nur deswegen so, weil du generell Probleme mit der Rhetorik hast, weil sie nicht allein auf Logik aufbaut. Oder?"

„Überhaupt nicht. Ich traue nur dem ganzen Konzept nicht."

„Warum nicht? Rhetorik ist Kunst."

Nach einer kleinen Pause kam die Antwort. „Das ist keine Kunst. Natur ist Kunst, Lyrik ist Kunst. Kunst muss nicht überzeugen. Rhetorik ist Kenntnis. In Kenntnissen kannst du beides finden: Gunst und Unheil. Handelte es sich nicht um kenntnisreiche Rhetorik (mit

---

[3] Timocreon von Rhodes um 480 v. Chr.
[4] Wikipedia.org, Timocreon
[5] Aeschines. *Politiker und Redner*

ihrem praktischen Wissen, den gebildeten Gefühlen und der Projektion auf ein faszinierendes Bild) mit der das 'abgefeimteste aller wilden Tiere Gottes' Adam und Eva mit den unsterblichen Worten überzeugt hat: '... und ihr werdet sein wie Gott und wissen was Gut und was Böse ist'?[6] Das hat sich nicht gerade als wohltuend für sie herausgestellt."

„Und für die ganze Menschheit auch nicht, aber das ist ja auch nur eine Metapher."

„Na und?"

„Eine Metapher ist nicht real. Deswegen heißt sie ja Metapher."

„So, du beanspruchst Rhetorik also als nicht real, oder?„

„Ich weiß nicht. Ich denke, es geht nicht um real oder nicht. Du wirst es nicht gern hören

mögen. Aber das Gehirn kann nicht unterscheiden zwischen dem, was es um sich herum sieht oder an was es sich erinnert."

„Um Himmels willen, nun kommst du schon wieder damit – deinem Elfenbeinturm vom Glauben an geistige Bedeutung. Mein Glaube ist, was ich sehen kann und was ich anfassen kann, das ist real."

„Das ist aber nicht zu Ende gedacht. Realität ist vielschichtig, und es ist nicht leicht, sie eindeutig zu beobachten. Wenn du das nicht kannst, können deine Wahrnehmungen widersprüchlich sein und zu Konflikten führen. Dann ist es besser, diejenigen, die mit deinen Wahrnehmungen nicht übereinstimmen, respektvoll zu begegnen. Das ist das Ziel der Rhetorik. Ihre Bedeutung liegt in der idealisierten Gestaltung des Denkens, um zu einer entgegenkommenden und ehrlichen Debatte zu gelangen. Dabei sind geistige oder körperliche Verletzungen zu vermeiden, auch wenn es um den Erhalt berechtigter Standpunkte geht. Rhetoriker betrachten ihre Angelegenheiten sorgfältig. Das führt zu freundlichen statt zu streitsüchtigen Debatten, in denen sich dein Gegenüber somit deinen Wahrnehmungen öffnet, anstatt sich von ihnen verletzt oder in die Defensive gedrängt zu fühlen. Deswegen nenne ich das Kunst. Und ich bin nicht der Einzige. Nachdem die ‚Alten Griechen' Rhetorik entwickelten, wurden deren Ideen und Theorien von den römischen und den mittelalterlichen Intellektuellen übernommen und modifiziert."

„Ich weiß das schon. Aber was passiert in dem Fall, dass ein Redner einfach nur versucht zu gewinnen, um des Gewinnens wegen? Du kannst meinen Ansatz nicht wirklich zurückweisen, dass es ihm nicht um die Wahrheit geht, oder die beste Lösung, oder die sinnvollste Schlussfolgerung. Idealismus erfordert einen aufgeschlossenen Geist. Falls die Disputanten darauf vorbereitet sind, ihre Meinung zu ändern, wenn die Behauptungen sorgfältig gegeneinander abgewogen wurden, mögen die Aussichten ziemlich gut sein,

---

[6] *Genesis* 3:1-24

dass die beste Ansicht sich durchsetzt. Aber wenn es nur ums Gewinnen geht? Die Gesprächspartner könnten trügerisch vorgehen, sodass, wenn die Debatte vorüber ist, keiner weiß, ob die Schlussfolgerung aufgrund der besseren Argumente erfolgte oder ganz einfach nur auf der Grundlage eines miesen Tricks."

„Ja gut, aber dann ist es keine Rhetorik, sondern Betrug."

„Natürlich ist es das. Und schau dir die 'abgefeimte Kreatur' in der Genesis an. Sie wurde deshalb für das, was sie getan hatte, zum Leben als Schlange verurteilt. Aber darum geht es nicht. Es geht um den in der Tat vorhandenen schmalen Grat zwischen: einen Fall gewinnen um des Gewinnens oder um der Wahrheit willen. Dieser schmale Grat kann darüber entscheiden, ob jemand ein Held wird oder ein Tyrann."

Sie schwiegen eine Weile, erhoben sich dann von ihrer Bank und gingen über den Strand zum Wasser. Sie wanderten die Küste in südliche Richtung entlang und verloren sich in Gedanken über die Gestalten der Mythologien aus aller Welt und darüber, dass Helden, als Symbole der

Wahrheit, nur versinnbildlicht erscheinen können. Dass sie kosmische Energien sind, die als zauberhafte Töne in das menschliche Bewusstsein ausstrahlen und unsere Welt mit Vorstellungen, Wahrnehmungen, Erfahrungen und Einstellungen erfüllen. Sie dachten auch daran, dass die Bedeutungen leider unübersichtlich geworden sind, wie Sigmund Freud es im Zusammenhang mit den Religionen einmal darstellte:

Die Wahrheiten, welche die religiösen Lehren enthalten, sind doch so entstellt und systematisch verkleidet, daß die Masse der Menschen sie nicht als Wahrheit erkennen kann. Es ist ein ähnlicher Fall, wie wenn wir dem Kind erzählen, daß der Storch die Neugeborenen bringt. Auch damit sagen wir die Wahrheit in symbolischer Verhüllung, denn wir wissen, was der große Vogel bedeutet. Aber das Kind weiß es nicht, es hört nur den Anteil der Entstellung heraus, hält sich für betrogen, und wir wissen, wie oft sein Mißtrauen gegen die Erwachsenen und seine Widersetzlichkeit gerade an diesen Eindruck anknüpft. Wir sind zur Überzeugung gekommen, daß es besser ist, die Mitteilung solcher symbolischer Verschleierungen der Wahrheit zu unterlassen und dem Kind die Kenntnis der realen Verhältnisse in Anpassung an seine intellektuelle Stufe nicht zu versagen.[7]

Die Wahrheit zu entdecken, wissen die Wanderer, kann nur so betrachtet werden, dass man hinter die Mythen schaut, ähnlich wie wenn man den Ideen oder Vorstellungen eines Dichters nachspüren wollte, obwohl sie sich nicht vollständig enthüllen lassen. Doch die Wahrheit ist in uns. Die kosmische oder göttliche Energie ist in unserem Geist verborgen. Wenn wir tief genug hinabsteigen, mögen wir einen dieser Helden aus unseren

---

[7] Sigmund Freud. *Die Zukunft einer Illusion*. Standard Edit., Kapitel 8.

W.A.R. ~ *We Are Revolution*

Mythologien finden, unseren 'Retter aus der Not' im Angesicht von Trauer und Leid. Die Wahrheit von Erlösung und Wiedergeburt, wie wir sie in all den kleinen Wiedergeburten innerhalb unseres Lebens finden, ist nur als eine Metapher vorstellbar, als ein Bild, symbolisiert in Geschichten: Maria und Josef, Unbefleckte Empfängnis, Asyl, Kreuzigung, Auferstehung und Himmelfahrt: Das alles sind Störche.

So wandern sie den sonnigen Strand entlang, ohne viel um sich herum zu bemerken. Einen von ihnen bekümmern gar die Strahlen der Sonne nicht, denn er trägt seinen Hut in der Hand. In Gedanken ist er bei der Suche nach einer Antwort auf die Bemerkung darüber, jemand würde entweder ein Held oder Tyrann werden. Schließlich sagt er: „Schau, du kannst eine anerkannte Kunst nicht verurteilen wegen der Annahme, sie könne in übler Weise missbraucht werden. Grundsätzlich besteht sie weiterhin darin, Feindseligkeit, Misshandlung und Gewalt zu verhindern."

„Schöner Ansatz. Aber wie kannst du das wissen? Es gibt einen besseren Weg dafür, ohne dieses ganze ethische und emotionale Zeug einzusetzen."

„Gibt es?"

„Ja, Resolution."

„Resolution? Wie meinst du das?"

„Ich meine das im Sinne des Verfahrens aus der formalen Logik in dem das zuvor Behauptete widerlegt wird?"

„Aber das hat nach meinem Dafürhalten viel mehr Potenzial für einen Wettbewerb, der zu gewinnen ist."

„Vielleicht, aber selbst wenn, es ist dann aber wenigstens ein offensichtlicher. Beide Parteien wissen, oder könnten wissen, was die wahre Absicht ist. Sie haben dieselben Chancen zu gewinnen, und der Gewinner würde nicht beanspruchen, ein besserer Sprecher zu sein."

„Das verstehe ich. Von deinem Standpunkt aus gesehen reicht es, Logik in die Debatte einzubringen. Du denkst, all das ethische und emotionale Zeug, wie du es so schön gesagt hast, sei etwas, wie – sagen wir mal – in die Ferien zu fahren, wo du Menschlichkeit genießen kannst, ohne darüber nachdenken zu müssen. Dabei vernachlässigst du etwas, das du genauso gut weißt wie ich, nämlich, wenn wir sprechen, um andere zu überzeugen, wissen wir niemals ob unsere Wörter denselben Sinn haben wie die Wörter der anderen, oder anders ausgedrückt, ob wir dieselbe Sprache sprechen."

Es hatte aber alle Welt einerlei Zunge und Sprache. Da sie nun zogen gen Morgen, fanden sie ein ebenes Land im Lande Sinear, und wohnten daselbst. Und sie sprachen untereinander:... Wohlauf, laßt uns eine Stadt und einen Turm bauen, dessen Spitze bis an den Himmel reiche, daß wir uns einen Namen machen! denn wir werden sonst zerstreut in alle Länder. Da fuhr der HERR hernieder, daß er sähe die Stadt und den Turm, die die Menschenkinder bauten. Und der HERR sprach: Siehe, es ist einerlei Volk und einerlei Sprache unter ihnen allen, und haben das angefangen zu tun; sie werden nicht ablassen von allem, was sie sich vorgenommen haben zu tun. Wohlauf, laßt uns herniederfahren und ihre Sprache daselbst verwirren, daß keiner des andern Sprache verstehe! Also zerstreute sie der HERR von dort in alle Länder, daß sie mußten aufhören die Stadt zu bauen. Daher heißt ihr Name Babel, daß der HERR daselbst verwirrt hatte aller Länder Sprache und sie zerstreut von dort in alle Länder.[8]

Das ging den Wanderern bei dem Begriff „dieselbe Sprache„, sofort durch den Kopf; der bekannte Mythos darüber, wie die unterschiedlichen Sprachen in die Welt kamen. Er symbolisiert den Verlust des Ursprünglichen, das aus unserem inneren Fühlen entstand und entsprechend der spirituellen Belange gesprochen wurde. Es ist bekannt, dass das antike Semitisch ohne Vokale geschrieben wurde und die Konsonanten allein die Wurzeln des Wortes bedeuteten. Die Konsonanten gaben dem Wort einen Sinn, die Vokale gestalteten es mit bestimmten Erfahrungswerten. Dabei erinnerten die Wanderer auch, was der schwedische Philosoph Emanuel Swedenborg in diesem Zusammenhang sagte: *Jeder Teil eines Wortes besteht aus einem eigenen Sinn der die Dinge spirituell und himmlisch behandelt, nicht*

natürlich und weltlich wie sie im Sinne der Buchstaben behandelt werden.[9]

Das bedeutet, als die Menschen in der Sprache den höheren Sinn vernachlässigten, der die Naturgesetze vermittelte, verflüchtigte sich auch ihre Verbundenheit mit der spirituellen Welt. Es entwickelten sich tausende von verschiedenen Sprachen. Seitdem spricht alle Welt nicht mehr mit „einerlei Zunge und Sprache".

Derjenige von den beiden, der gerade das mit 'derselben Sprache' aufgebracht hatte, erläuterte: „Betrachtet man den Indo-Europäischen Sprachenbaum mit seinen verschiedenen Ästen von Sprachen, ob heutzutage ausgestorben oder noch am Leben, fällt es nicht leicht, diesen Gedanken zu verstehen. Deshalb besteht eher die Bereitschaft, die Idee der ganz offensichtlichen 'Sprachverwirrung' zu akzeptieren. Im Kern bedeutet 'dieselbe Sprache' das Sprechen in der Bedeutung des Wortes. Der alte Begriff von der ‚Sprache des Herzens' wurde in verständliche Sprache übersetzt, in die ‚Sprache des Gehirns'. Ein Ergebnis davon ist, das viele Dinge, die evident für die Menschen früherer Zeiten waren, vor uns verborgen bleiben. Sprache vermittelt nur noch Gedanken, außer in Lyrik und Kunst. Das mag einer der Gründe sein, weshalb es so schwierig ist, Lyrik in

---

8 *Genesis* 11:1–9
9 Himmel und Hölle, 1-4 von Emanuel Swedenborg, [1758]

einer anderen als der eigenen Muttersprache zu schreiben. Im ersten Fall kommt die Sprache aus dem Gehirn und im zweiten aus dem Herzen."

„Hm, hm" murmelte der Begleiter. Doch der Sprecher ließ sich nicht unterbrechen: „Sprache ist auch die Basis für das grundsätzliche Menschenrecht der Freiheit des Wortes. Das Recht beansprucht, und beansprucht nur, Regierungen an Vergeltung, Zensur oder sozialen Zwangsmaßnahmen zu hindern, damit keiner in Furcht leben muss. Das heißt allerdings nicht, dass jeder sagen kann, was er oder sie möchte. Selbst Schriftsteller und Journalisten, für die es der bedeutsamste Teil ihrer Arbeit ist, können dies nicht. Es ist nämlich noch ein anderes Menschenrecht involviert, das beansprucht, das alle Menschen frei und gleich an Würde und Rechten geboren sind und sich einander im Geist der Brüderlichkeit begegnen sollen."

„Ach, das nun wieder. Der Geist der Brüderlichkeit. Ist das nicht nur ein anderer Mythos?"

„Nein, ist es nicht. Es ist eine der bedingungslosen Wahrheiten, die C. G. Jung meinte, als er begründete, dass, und ich zitiere: ‚Alles was uns an anderen irritiert, führt uns zu einem Verständnis unserer selbst'. Das ist im Übrigen auch das Konzept von Achtsamkeit und Mitgefühl in der Buddhistischen Lehre, dem Dharma. Eine der fundamentalen Schritte, um Erleuchtung zu erlangen, ist die Idee der Rechten Rede. Nicht nur die richtigen Dinge zu sagen, also nicht zu lügen, sondern auch die Worte sorgsam abzuwägen, um jede Art von Ärgernis zu vermeiden. Mitgefühl im Dharma bedeutet: was einem anderen geschieht, auch dir selbst passieren kann. Deshalb beinhaltet das Menschenrecht auf Freiheit des Wortes eben auch, Worte sehr achtsam zu gebrauchen. Ein gesprochenes Wort, wie es ein muslimischer Kalif[10] einst gesagt haben soll, ist eines der drei Dinge im Leben, die man nicht rückgängig machen kann."

„Ja, ich denke, das ist richtig. Obwohl ich nicht so sicher bin mit der Zahl drei. Wie auch immer, was ich als gesunden Menschenverstand ansehe, ist Anstand. Dazu gehört, sehr sorgfältig zu überlegen, bevor man spricht oder schreibt, ansonsten kann man leicht Unheil anrichten."

„Du hast Recht. Selbst Poeten müssen in dieser Weise ihre Worte betrachten, auch wenn sie nicht beabsichtigen, Schaden anzurichten."

Die Wanderer stimmten darin überein, dass Dichter nur beabsichtigen, ihre Bilder in Worte kleiden; sonst nichts. Dennoch müssen sie dabei achtsam sein. In diesem Zusammenhang priesen sie den amerikanischen Schriftsteller, Ernest Hemingway, mit seiner ‚Eisberg-Theorie'. Sie besagt, je weniger Worte ein Schriftsteller verwendet, umso mehr Raum lässt

---

10 Caliph Umar, ca. 577 bis 644; Drei Dinge kannst du niemals zurücknehmen: einen geworfenen Speer, ein gesprochenes Wort und eine vergebene Gelegenheit.

er dem Leser, um das bestimmte Bild zu finden:

Wenn ein Schriftsteller genügend darüber weiß, über was er schreibt, mag er Dinge auslassen, die er und der Leser kennen. Wenn der Schriftsteller ehrlich genug schreibt, wird er so starke Gefühle über diese Dinge vermitteln, als wenn er sie beschrieben hätte.[11]

„Lass mich mal so fragen: Ist es nicht die Kardinalfrage, warum Worte, Sprache und Rede verletzen können, wenn sie nur von einer einzigen Person kommen und auch nur mit dieser Person zu tun haben?"

„Ja, genau das ist sie, und zwar deshalb, weil sie heutzutage nicht aus dem Geist heraus kommen, sondern allein aus dem Gehirn. Der Sprache mangelt es an Bildern und sie manipuliert. Es fehlt der Geist der Brüderlichkeit. Denk an C. G. Jung und seine Idee der *Archetypen des Kollektiven Unbewussten*. Psychoanalytiker wie er haben unseren Verstand geöffnet, um unsere Herzen zu ergründen, wie es der amerikanische Wissenschaftler und Schriftsteller Joseph Campbell bezeichnet hat. Er beschrieb, dass Sigmund Freuds kühne und wahrhaftig epochemachende Schriften der Psychoanalyse unverzichtbar sind, um die Mythologien zu verstehen, und was man von den detaillierten und manchmal widersprüchlichen Interpretationen bestimmter Fälle und Probleme halten kann. *Freud, Jung und ihre Anhänger haben unwiderlegbar das Überleben der Logik, der Helden und der Taten des Mythos bis hinein in die heutige Zeit gezeigt. In Abwesenheit einer wirksamen allgemeinen Mythologie hat jeder von uns sein privates, unerkanntes, rudimentäres, doch heimlich wirksames Pantheon des Traums. Die neueste Inkarnation des Ödipus, die fortbestehende Romantik von Die Schöne und das Biest, steht heute Nachmittag an der Ecke der 44. Straße und der 5. Avenue und wartet darauf, dass die Ampel umspringt.*[12] Ich verstehe es so, dass der Kampf zwischen dem Ego und dem Sein in der Tiefe des Unbekannten zurückgelassen ist. Jede Person hat das Verhältnis zur Umwelt und den Bedingungen, um sie herum zu beobachten, um seinen oder ihren Platz in der Welt von Zeit und Raum zu finden."

„Ist das nicht ein bisschen viel verlangt für jeden einzelnen Menschen?"

"Nein, ist es nicht. Entsprechend der Lehre des deutschen Philosophen Arthur Schopenhauer hat jeder an dem Platz in der Welt zu leben, den er für sich gefunden hat. Der „Welt der Vorstellungen", wie er seine Idee von der Welt unseres Bewusstseins nennt. Entweder durch aktives Interesse oder passiven Konsum; die Antwort darauf, wer wir sind, ist nur durch Gefühl oder Erfahrung zu erreichen. Nicht hilfreich sind religiöse Konzepte, die mythologische Beschreibungen für selbstverständlich halten oder Erkenntnisse der Wissenschaft, die den Geist der Mythologie ignorieren und die Rationalität als einzige

---

[11] Ernest Hemingway in *Tod am Nachmittag*
[12] Campbell, Der Held in tausend Gestalten, Prolog

Grundlage anerkennen. Obwohl einige wissenschaftliche Konzepte durchaus die alten Weisheiten unterstützen, wie man beispielsweise an der Urknalltheorie sieht, die in der Tradition des spirituellen Konzepts der Trennung steht. Aber im Allgemeinen ist die Wissenschaft gescheitert, die Mythologie zu ersetzen und eine Welt anzubieten, die allein auf dem Verstand basiert. In dem Chaos der „Welt der Vorstellungen,„ in der die Menschen leben, mag es deshalb vorkommen, dass einige überhaupt keine Antwort finden und im Dunkel des Unbekannten bleiben."

„Ich will dir mal nicht widersprechen, weil ich uns nicht den Nachmittag verderben möchte und weil ich weiß, dass du nicht viel vom Verstand hältst."

„Oh, warum nicht? . . . Aber danke."

Unsere Wanderer geben einstweilen ihre Gedanken auf und erfreuen sich ihres Weges auf dem fast menschenleeren Strand, der mit abertausenden der kleinen ägäischen Kieselsteine bedeckt ist, welche die Füße beim Wandern so angenehm massieren. Kleine Wellen, immer noch voll Seegras und mit Treibholz nach dem Gewitter der letzten Nacht, spülen seicht ans Land. Eine erfrischende Brise schwingt durch die Luft. Obwohl bereits Herbst, glüht die Sonne sommerlich. Von fern grüßt die Wandersleute eine bizarre kleine Bergkette und hinter dem Wasser der Ägäis, rechts von ihnen, erhebt sich die wesentlich höhere der türkischen Küste.

Plötzlich, stelle dir vor, hier, an diesem Strand oder woanders auf einer anderen griechischen Insel, stelle dir vor, einen kleinen dunklen Punkt auf dem Wasser. Doch sich das vorzustellen ist nicht wirklich nötig. Heutzutage wird alles im Fernsehen gezeigt oder den Sozialen Netzwerken vertrieben. Die Welt ist geschrumpft. Alles ist sichtbar geworden.

Der kleine Punkt wird größer und größer. Menschen in einem Boot. Einem kleinen Boot. Sie jubeln, als sie Strand erreichen. Erleichtert. Andere, zu anderen Gelegenheiten, in anderen Booten, jubeln nicht. Sie haben ihre Kraft verloren. Einige ihrer Begleiter gar in den Wellen des Meeres. Aber alle entsteigen ihren Booten und steigen auf in ihren Hoffnungen.

Europäische Sonnenanbeter, im Vergnügen unbeschwerter Ferien, sind mit Menschen aus Asien und Arabien konfrontiert, die erschöpft, hungrig und verzweifelt an den Stränden der ägäischen Inseln erscheinen – und den Touristen das Ferienvergnügen rauben.

Je mehr Flüchtlinge erscheinen, desto weniger Touristen kommen und lassen die Einheimischen ohne Einnahmen und in wachsendem Dilemma. Lassen sie allein mit traumatisierten Kindern und Erwachsenen, die aus überfüllten, kaum seetauglichen Booten steigen, die bereits fast in dem Moment zu sinken begannen, als sie die türkische Küste verließen. Sie erreichten mühsam das ‚Gelobte Land' mit nicht viel mehr als einer Plastiktüte für ihre Habseligkeiten, wenn überhaupt. Betraten eine Zukunft für sich selbst, in der sie Geld verdienen und ihre Familien daheim unterstützen wollten.

Sie kamen aus Gegenden voller Feindseligkeit und Gewalt. Überwanden Hindernisse entlang ihres teilweise jahrelangen Flüchtlingspfads. Marschierten hunderte Kilometer durch schroffe fremdartige Landschaften. Gaben all ihr Geld allein um das Land zu finden, von dem sie träumten, das jedoch auf sie nicht vorbereitet war.

Eine riesige Zahl Frieden suchender Menschen. Nachdem sie angelangt waren, mussten sie in langen Reihen anstehen, um sich registrieren zu lassen, um ein Ticket für eine der Schiffsfähren auf das Festland zu erhalten, das nur nach der Registrierung erworben werden konnte. Wenn es überhaupt welche geben sollte. Oder sie belegten Lager, warteten auf Asyl, auf Obdach, Nahrung, Arbeit, warteten auf ein Leben. Abertausende. Und sie waren nicht die einzigen: andere erreichten Europa auf dem Landweg und somit ging die Zahl der Flüchtlinge in die Millionen.

Wenn die beiden Wanderer an die jetzige Situation denken, sind sie sich einig darüber, dass die Geschichte voll ist mit Flucht und Vertreibung, und mit Konflikten in Gegenden, in welche sich die Menschen in großer Zahl flüchteten. Diese Menschen hier in der Ägäis kamen aus Angst. Aber die Europäer sind ebenfalls voller Furcht. Ihre Ablehnung, die sie zu großen Teilen den Flüchtlingen gegenüber entwickeln, steht für diese Furcht. Sie basiert auf dem Unbekannten, dem Unvorhergesehenen, dem Irrationalen – besteht in einem Wort aus: Unbeständigkeit.

„Unbeständigkeit,„ sagt einer der Wanderer, „ist der übliche Zustand der Dinge. Hier führt sie zu einer übermäßigen Angst. Sie entstammt der Vorstellung, wonach so vielen Flüchtlingen keine Unterkunft und Verpflegung gewährt werden kann, wie sie erwartet wird, ohne dass man selbst erheblich darunter leiden wird. Es ist der Glaube, wenn die Flüchtlinge nicht zurückgewiesen werden, an den Verlust alles Erreichten und der bekannten Lebensumstände. Eine Glaube, geboren aus der Vorstellung: ‚Dann werden wir alle sterben'. Furcht, wie Ablehnung selbst (oder ihr Gegenteil: Verlangen), ist vom Verstand gesteuert. Es hat für mich etwas von einem charakterlichen Reflex. Insofern ist die Furcht ein Teil der menschlichen Natur, der auf Ablehnung basiert. Obwohl Furcht oder Angst als eine Art Regulativ im Leben wirken können, werden sie gefährlich, wenn sie als überwertig empfunden werden. Doch wenn der Verstand nicht von überwertiger Furcht beherrscht wird, macht sich ein anderer archetypischer Reflex im Menschen bemerkbar, wenn die Situation es erfordert. Es ist das Mitgefühl."

„Ja, ich schätze, du kannst das so nennen. Soweit ich weiß, hat es sich auch deutlich gezeigt. Dennoch haben die europäischen Staaten Griechenland allein gelassen, als abertausende von Flüchtlingen die Ägäis überquerten. All die Flüchtlinge, in endlosen

Reihen vor dem Registrationsbüro und auf der Suche nach Obdach und Nahrung, hat die Regierung des Landes überfordert. Dafür waren dann die Bewohner der Inseln da und Leute von außerhalb, die zur Hilfe kamen, sogar einige Touristen halfen, auch wenn es das Geringste war, was sie tun konnten in der Situation."

„Da hast du Recht. Aber wenn wir bei der Regierung sind, dann ist sie für Mitgefühl nicht zuständig. Es ist es gerade der Sinn des Mitgefühls, dass sie in der Aufmerksamkeit der Menschen erwacht, nicht in der von Institutionen. Das Fehlen von Mitgefühl insofern, ist das Fehlen des Mitgefühls der Menschen, die leider hinter den Institutionen stehen. Denen war und ist nicht bewusst, dass, was dem einen passieren kann, auch dem anderen geschehen mag. Was dir passiert, passiert auch mir. Die Welt ist ständig in Bewegung, *panta rhei*.[13] Jeder ist mit jedem verbunden. All das Leben und all das Leid. Denen hat sich die Gewissheit nicht erschlossen, die uns tief aus unserem Unbewussten erreicht. Die Gewissheit: Wenn du leidest, leide ich."

Auf ihrem Weg sprachen die beiden weiterhin über die Situation auf den ägäischen Inseln, auf denen an manchen Tagen mehr als fünftausend Flüchtlinge landeten, meistens nass bis auf die Knochen, durstig und hungrig. Die meisten hatten alles verloren, bis auf ihr Geschichten. Mitten unter ihnen, an den Stränden, die gesprenkelt waren mit Schwimmwesten, Booten und Gerümpel, konnte man Helfer sehen mit Wasser, Nahrungsmitteln und Kleidung. Nicht genug natürlich. Aber eine Gottesgabe für die Ankommenden. Die Helfer gaben alles, was sie hatten, ertrugen den Verlust der Einnahmen der ausbleibenden Touristen und tolerierten Lager voller verzweifelter Flüchtlinge in ihrer Nachbarschaft. Diese Einwohner, die taten, was sie glaubten tun zu müssen, gab es überall in Europa. Wenn diese Helfer gefragt wurden, warum sie das machten, dann antworteten sie: „Was sonst können wir tun?"

Aber es waren auch jene zu finden, die von überwertiger Angst getrieben, Flüchtlingsheime niederbrannten, Ankömmlinge bedrohten und Demonstrationen gegen sie veranstalteten. Die den Flüchtlingen die Schuld gaben, für alles, was ihrer Meinung nach nicht richtig war. Kaltblütige Politiker nutzten die Gelegenheit, und betrachteten sie als ein Geschenk des Himmels. Mit simplen Argumenten versuchten sie zu überzeugen, dass an allem Leid der Welt die Flüchtlinge (und die Globalisierung) schuld seien.

„Was glaubst du, wie die armen Flüchtlinge sich fühlten," fragte einer der Wanderer, „wenn sie diese Anfeindungen hörten und erneut mit einer Situation konfrontiert waren, vor der sie doch geflohen waren: Hass und Unglück."

„Ungerecht behandelt, würde ich annehmen. Aber, andere für unerfüllte Träume und Wünsche zu beschuldigen, auch wenn es sich bei ihnen um unrealistische oder

---

13 Heraclitus von Ephesus, Griechischer Philosoph, ca. 535 bis 475 v. Chr.

ungewöhnliche Erwartungen handelt, ist üblich. Denke beispielsweise zurück an Deutschland in 1933. Damals waren es ‚die Juden und die Verträge von Versailles'."

„Du hast Recht. Diese Ankläger können nicht nachvollziehen, was es ist, das die Helfer geleitet hat, und sie hassen die Politiker, die den Flüchtlingen Schutz gewährt haben. Für diese Menschen, die von ihrer überwertigen Angst getrieben werden, gibt es nur eine Lösung, nämlich Ablehnung und die Sehnsucht danach, die Flüchtlinge wieder loszuwerden, statt sie zu beherbergen, ihnen Schutz in ihrer Hilflosigkeit zu gewähren oder Trost in ihrer Verzweifelten zu spenden."

„Das habe ich verstanden. Doch andererseits: Auch wenn ich glaube, du liegst mit all dem, was du vom Mitgefühl sagst, richtig. Aber es ist nicht die alleinige Lösung in diesem Problem. Ich denke, die Menschen agieren nicht gänzlich falsch – natürlich meine ich nicht die gewaltsamen Formen. Falls du Zweifel daran hast, ob du in der Lage bist, Millionen von Flüchtlingen zu beherbergen und zu verpflegen, würde es nicht fahrlässig sein, sogar unter dem Eindruck Migration zu vermeiden, nicht dem Verstand zu folgen?"

„Selbstverständlich wäre es das. Der Verstand ist dazu da, rational und vernünftig zu handeln. Das Problem ist der Konflikt. Die Erkenntnis, dass allein vom Herzen oder allein vom Verstand geführte Handlungen weder spirituell noch vernünftig sind, steckt ursprünglich innerhalb eines jeden menschlichen Wesens."

„So, wir kommen also zurück zu unserem nagenden Problem, dass die Menschen sich untereinander nicht verstehen, oder?"

„Ja, schau was in den Ländern, von denen die Flüchtlinge als „Gelobtes Land" träumen passiert ist, wenn sie mit Ablehnung reagierten. Dort dachten die Menschen an die steigende Zahl von ihnen, die in Armut leben und wegen der sinkenden Stellenangebote auf Sozialleistungen angewiesen sind. Arme und unbeschäftigte Menschen leben in problematischen Wohngebieten. Sehen sich einer hohen Zahl von Schulabrechern oder geringeren Bildungschancen gegenüber. Eine bedeutende Anzahl der Jugendlichen sind ohne jede Chance auf eine Arbeitsstelle. Es ist kein Wunder, dass als Realität hauptsächlich mangelnde Unterstützung und Vorabendserien im Fernsehen wahrgenommen werden."

„Und nicht zu vergessen: Nachrichtenkanäle. Wenn du ständig Horden von fremdartig aussehenden Menschen gezeigt bekommst, die Strände stürmen oder durch Zäune brechen, sind das die Bilder der Realität. Aber man sieht nur, was man sehen will. Die andere Realität, die Verzweiflung und Aussichtslosigkeit der Emigranten, sieht man nicht. Es stimmt, Flüchtlinge sind nicht eingeladen. Sie kommen einfach – mit leeren Händen ohne den geringsten Plan. Ihr Effekt ist der, dass sie das soziale Leben der gastgebenden Gesellschaften stören. Aber sie kommen, nachdem sie gezwungen waren, ihre eigene Angst zu überwinden."

W.A.R. ~ *We Are Revolution*

„Richtig, nun tu mir den Gefallen und stelle dir ein Bild vor, das nicht nur Teile beschreibt, sondern die ganze Realität. Ich möchte nicht überheblich sein – aber du musst nicht nur die richtigen Worte finden, sondern auch ihre Bedeutungen; nicht nur die Logik in ihnen, sondern auch den Geist."

„Du meinst einen neuen Helden?"

„Ja."

Sie wandern weiter die Küste entlang, beide gedankenversunken und in stillschweigender Überzeugung, dass es das Beste ist, gemeinsam zu wandern.

Essays, Critiques and Creative Prose

> STUDENT
> Yet in the word must some idea be
> MEPHISTOPHELES
> Of course! But only shun too over-sharp a tension
> For just where fails the comprehension
> A word steps promptly in as deputy
> *Faust I, Scene IV, The Study*

Wayfarers
Gino Leineweber

Two wayfarers walk. Sometimes together in peace and quiet. Sometimes not. Imagine them as 'grumpy old men', or as competitors, or as two long-time companions that either feel attracted to or contradict each other. Anyway, it is not easy to discern the bonds that bind them, but they give the impression that they are somehow tied to each other.

We now follow them coming down the three hundred and fifty steps from the tiny, Byzantine church of Tsambika Monastery Cathedral perched high at three hundred meters on the top of a hill with a remarkable view over the Aegean Sea. They are on their way from Lindos to Rhodes City and curious about the energy of a place that, as the legend puts it, will bless with children any woman with fertility problems that climbs up there to pray to the Virgin Mary.

Both of them are talking calmly, which might indicate a topic of conversation concerning which their opinions are in agreement about. The one guided by his heart believes that nobody knows what kind of energy really surrounds us all and that there might be one that has the power to effect a change in a human being with a certain prayer while the other, guided by his brain, thinks that there is only one way of conceiving a child, and that is not brought about by praying. Today both of them actually want to walk together, but you never know: when it comes to a difference of opinion, they sometimes part, each cursing the other.

However, the beauty of Rhodes, with its abundance of nature, the rugged landscape lovingly covered with pine and cypress forests, with vineyards and remarkable olive trees, has created a tranquil mood in them, motivating them to share their thoughts. Even ruins enhance the beauty of the landscape. They got that impression when, on their trip, they arrived at the so-called Villa Mussolini. It was supposed to be the venue for the Italian dictator when he would stay in Greece after the intended winning of the war. As everyone knows, there was no victory. He never laid his head to rest in that region. He missed a wonderful view: beautiful hills and valleys right down to the Aegean. Now it is moldering away. But the partly destroyed walls, windows, doors and roofs make art of it, render it aesthetic, highlighted with the graffiti on the bright blue-yellow walls. And the beauty is also in the ruins of the ancient buildings like acropolises and fortresses. Although the influence of tourism cannot be ignored, the island is characterized by the legacy of its history, not least the buildings and, in a way, the people's hospitality too. For example;

after crossing a ridge of mountains with many caves below the peaks, called the Caves of St. George, the wanderers experience the latter when stopping by for a cold drink in the little taverna next to a small chapel.

It is a sunny afternoon. The innkeepers, a couple with a little daughter, cater to them besides the drinks with some appetizers on the house.

After arriving in Rhodes City, they sat on a bench on the sidewalk across from the tavern Ateya. It was named for the owner, a native of Egypt, who served them some fresh seafood the previous night. He barbecued it directly in front of the venue, actually on the street, right in front of a remarkable sunset on the horizon.

One of the wayfarers now points at a sculpture in the middle of a roundabout to their left and says:

"Do you know what that is?"

"Of course, I do. It's Diagoras of Rhodes, carried by two of his sons on their shoulders. He was one of the heroes of Rhodes."

"Yes," replies the other, "it's quite the island of giants and heroes here", and they start to talk about this.

First of all, of course, there is the Colossus of Rhodes, an artistic character dedicated to Helios, the great god of Rhodes. He was and is the most famous. As a matter of fact, he owes his fame to his former monument. It was considered one of the Seven Wonders of the World.

"Let's think about the human heroes these islands once had: there was Leonidas of Rhodes, the most famous ancient Olympic runner, who, for four consecutive Olympiads,[1] captured the gold medal in three separate foot races."

"Yes," his companion laughs, "can you imagine? This ancient record was just broken for the first time in 2016 by the American Michael Phelps. More than 2,000 years later." He shakes his head in disbelief and continues: "Leonidas might have been running in the very stadium in the ancient Acropolis of Rhodes that we passed on our way yesterday."

"Of course, he would have. When we were resting there on the stages, I imagined a race, a stadium, which, as you know, used to be the supreme discipline of the Olympic games. In my mind's eye, Leonidas started quickly amidst a crowd of nearly twenty others, all of them stark naked, as was common then. I could clearly see his lead. So, the officials at the end had no problems pronouncing him the winner, whereupon the ecstatic crowd carried him on their shoulders to triumphant ovations."

"That's nice," came the reply, "but if you'd gone some centuries further back in your mind's eye, you might have seen Diagoras in a boxing match, most likely amidst thousands of euphoric people cheering him on. He was also known as Periodonikis, the period winner, and had next to Rhodes many other victories in local games: in Athens, Thebes, Argos, Megara, Aegina, and most importantly, he won at all the Greek games—at the Olympic Games, the Pythian Games, even four times at the Isthmian Games and twice

---

[1] 164-152 BCE

at the Nemean Games. And he was not only famous for his own victories but also for those of his family members."

He pointed again at the roundabout: "That sculpture actually shows it was 448 BC and Diagoras was already an old man when two of his sons were crowned Olympic victors on the same day . . ."

". . .Yes, I know," the other interrupted, "and while the masses cheered on, the sons lifted their father onto their shoulders. It is said that a Spartan stood up and shouted ‚Die now, Diagoras, you shall not become a God! "—meaning that he had reached the height of bliss that a mortal could receive upon earth. Actually, Diagoras died amidst the applause of the crowd that day."

"You know that, of course, but did you also know his fame was celebrated by the ancient Greek lyric poet Pindar?"[2]

"Of course, I do. But talking about heroes and poets, think about Timocreon."[3] Both were laughing because that poet was a giant not merely for his poetry, which survives only in a very few fragments; he was also outstanding just for having composed convivial verses for drinking parties. He distinguished himself as both athlete and glutton.

"Think about what happened at the court of the Persian king, where he was eating so much that the king himself asked him what he was trying to do. Timocreon replied he was getting ready to beat countless Persians and, the very next day, he did just that. After overpowering all who dared to fight him, he started punching the air just to show that "he had lots of fight left in him for anyone still wanting to take him on." [4]

"Where did you get that from?"

"The Greek rhetorician Athenaeus of Naukratios. Rhetoric, by the way, brings me to another historic figure I would call one of the heroes of Rhodes: Aeschines."

"Are you serious? He wasn't from Rhodes. He was from Athens."[5]

"That's right. Nevertheless, here it was that he opened a school of rhetoric. You might picture him before your imaginary eyes at the acropolis as well. You just have to go northwest from the Stadium to find the Odeon, where he might have held his lectures in front of an audience of about as many as eight hundred."

"Alas," the other gloomily replies, "I can't because, nothing now remains of that small marble theater. But, more critically, I wouldn't call a rhetorician a hero."

"That's because you have problems with rhetoric in general, it not being based on logic alone. Isn't that right?"

"No, I'm skeptical about the whole concept."

"Why? It's art."

After a little pause came the reply.

"No, it's not. Nature is art, poetry is art. Art doesn't need to convince. Rhetoric is

---

2 Thebes (Olympian Odes VII)
3 *Timocreon* of Rhodes about 480 BC
4 Wikipedia.org, Timocreon
5 *Aeschines*. A politician and orator, who went to Rhodes *c.*330 BC after a long – term quarrel with his colleague Demosthenes.

skill. In skills you can find both favor and harm. Was it not a skillful rhetoric (with its practiced knowledge, created emotions, and projection of a mesmerizing image) that enabled 'the more crafty than any of the wild animals of the Lord' to convince Adam and Eve with the immortal words: 'you will be like God knowing good and evil'?[6] It didn't turn out well for them."

"And not for the rest of mankind either, but it's still a metaphor."

"So what?"

"A metaphor isn't real. That's why it is a metaphor."

"You don't claim rhetoric to be real, do you?"

"I don't know. I think 'real' isn't what matters. You won't like hearing this, but the brain doesn't actually distinguish between what it sees in its environment and what it remembers of it."

"Oh, for goodness' sake… You with your 'ivory tower' of spiritual meanings and beliefs. My belief is that if I can see it and touch it, then it's real."

"That falls too short. Reality is versatile and it's not easy to observe it properly. If you don't, your perceptions are ambivalent and might lead to conflicts. It's better to treat those who disagree with your perceptions respectfully. That is the aim of rhetoric. It has its point in creating an idealistic configuration of thinking in terms of co-operative and honest debate. Nonetheless, to avoid mental and/or physical violation, rhetoric has legitimate points. Rhetors consider their concerns carefully. That leads to co-operative debates rather than confrontational ones. Your opponents become open to your opinions instead of feeling insulted and going on the defensive. That's why I call it an art. And I'm not the only one. After the philosophers of ancient Greece had developed it, the intellectuals of the Roman Empire and the medieval period adapted and modified Greek ideas and theories of rhetoric."

"I know, but what happens in the case of a debater, who simply gets to 'win' the argument for the sake of winning? You can't really deny he won't get to the truth, or the best solution, or the most logical conclusion. Idealism in a debate requires an open mind. If the disputants are prepared to change their minds after weighing the evidence carefully, the odds might be pretty good that the best case will prevail. But just to 'win'? Presenters can be deceptive so that, when the debate is over, you never know if the conclusion was the better argument or just a shifty trick."

"Then it isn't rhetoric, it's fraud."

"Of course, it is. But look at that crafty creature in Genesis. It was sentenced to remain a serpent for what it had done. But that's not the point. There is indeed a thin line between winning the case for the sake of winning or for the sake of truth. The thin line between becoming a hero or a tyrant."

They fell silent and after a while stood up from their bench. Going down to the beach. Following the seashore to the south. Walking away, preoccupied with the figures of mythology from all parts of the world. Heroes who appear as symbols of the truth can only

---

6 Genesis 3:1-24

be symbolized. It is a cosmic energy that emanates as a magic sound in the human consciousness and fills our world with beliefs, perceptions, experiences and conditions. They also thought that the meanings unfortunately became unclear, as Sigmund Freud once described it in connection with religions:

The truth is so distorted and systematically disguised that the mass of humanity cannot recognize as truth. The case is similar to what happens when we tell a child that newborn babies are brought by the stork. Here, too, we are telling the truth in symbolic clothing, for we know what the large bird signifies. But the child does not. It hears only the distorted part of what we say, and feels that it has been deceived; and we know how often its distrust of grown-ups and his refractoriness actually take their start from this impression. We have become convinced that it is better to avoid such symbolic disguising of the truth in what we tell children and not to withhold from them knowledge of the true state of affairs commensurate with their intellectual level.[7]

They think about to detecting the truth, and considering that, one has to go behind the myths. Similar as we have them in order to reveal an author's idea or imagery, although it not entirely possible. Yet the truth is inside us, that cosmic or divine energy is buried in our minds. If we go deep enough, we might find one of these heroes from our mythologies, as it were, 'the knight in shining armor' in the presence of grief and suffering. The truth of redemption and rebirth, as in all the little rebirths we face in our lifetime, is in our minds only imaginable for us as metaphors, symbolized in tales. Mary and Joseph, the Immaculate Conception, the Refuge, Crucifixion, Resurrection and Ascension: they are all storks.

So, they are walking down the sunny beach without noticing much around them. One of them has his summer hat in his hands, not being bothered by the glare of the sun. He is thinking of a reply to the other's statement about someone becoming either a hero or a tyrant. Finally, he says:

"Look, you can't blame an acknowledged art form only on the assumption it can be used in a bad way. The basic thing still remains that we avoid ill will, mistreatment and violence."

"Nice one, but how can you tell? There's a better way to avoid such things without employing all that ethical and emotional stuff."

"There is?"

"Yes, resolution."

"Resolution as in proposing, debating and resolving?"

"Yes."

"But that, in my opinion, has much more potential than a contest dedicated to winning."

"Maybe, but if so, it's at least an obvious one. Both parties know, or could know, what the true intention is, have the same chances of winning, and the winner wouldn't claim to be the better speaker."

"I can understand that, from your point of view, it is enough to introduce logic into

---

[7] Sigmund Freud. *Die Zukunft einer Illusion* Standard Edition, XXI; London: The Hogarth Press, 1961), pp. 44–45 (Orig. 19-27.)

the debate. You think, as you put it so simply, that all of "that ethical and emotional stuff" is something like being on a vacation, say, where you can enjoy humanity without thinking about it. You ignore something you know as well as I do, namely that, when writing or speaking to convince others of what we believe, we never know whether we're employing the same meaning in the words we use, the same language."

Once the whole earth had one language and the same words. As people migrated from the east, they found a plain in the land of Shinar and settled there. And they said to one another: ... "Come, let us build ourselves a city and a tower with its top in the heavens, and let us make a name for ourselves, lest we be dispersed over the face of the whole earth." And the Lord came down to see the city and the tower, which the children of man had built. And the Lord said, "Behold, they are one people, and they have all one language, and this is only the beginning of what they will do. And nothing that they propose to do will now be impossible for them. Come, let us go down and there confuse their language, so that they may not understand one another's speech." So, the Lord dispersed them from there over the face of all the earth, and they left off building the city. Therefore, its name was called Babel, because there the Lord confused the language of all the earth. And from there the Lord dispersed them over the face of all the earth.[8]

That immediately crossed their minds when mentioned the term "same language"; the famous myth of how the different languages came into the world symbolized the loss of the original that came out of inner feelings and was spoken according to spiritual settings. It is known that ancient Semitic was written without vowels and the meaning of the root is solely that of the consonants. The consonants gave a word meaning; the vowels invested a certain experience value. And thinking about that, they may remember the Swedish philosopher Emanuel Swedenborg, who in that regard said:

For in every particular of the Word there is an internal sense which treats of things spiritual and heavenly, not of things natural and worldly, such as are treated of in the sense of the letter.[9]

And that means, as men abandoned the greater sense that conveyed the law of nature, their affinity with the spiritual world also diminished to nothing. Languages have developed in their thousands since, and the whole earth no longer has 'one language and the same words'.

About the concept of 'same language', the wayfarer that has just brought it up, states: "Considering the Indo-European language tree with its different branches of languages, whether extinct nowadays or still alive, it is not easy to understand this notion; hence the readiness to accept the more obvious-looking notion of 'linguistic confusion'. At its core, however, is the speaking of the meaning of words—that 'same language'. The old expression of the 'language of the heart' was translated into a comprehensible language of the brain. As a result, it appears to have hidden many things from us that were evident to people in the past connected with nature and the spirit. Now, language expresses only

---

8 Genesis 11:1–9
9 *Heaven and Hell*, 1-4 by Emanuel Swedenborg, [1758], tr. by John C. Ager [1900] at sacred-texts.com

thoughts, except in poetry and art. And why is that? Because that origin is experience. It might be as well the reason that it is so difficult to create poetry in a language other than one's own. The former emerged from the brain, the latter from the heart."

"Hm, hm," a mumbled remark came. But the speaker did not let himself be interrupted: "Language, however, is as well the basis for the fundamental human right to freedom of speech. That right claims, and only claims, to prevent governmental retaliation, censorship, or societal sanction, so that no one needs fear. However, it does not mean someone can say whatever he or she like. Even writers and journalists, for whom it is the most significant part of their work, cannot. That is why there is another fundamental human right involved, which claims that all human beings are born free and equal in dignity and with fundamental rights and should act towards one another in a spirit of brotherhood."

"Oh, come on, the 'spirit of brotherhood'; isn't that just another myth?"

"No, it's not. It is one of the unconditional truths that C. G. Jung meant when he stated that, and I quote: "everything that irritates us about others can lead us to an understanding of ourselves, which, by the way, is the concept of mindfulness and compassion in Dharma, the Buddhist teaching, as well. One of the fundamental steps to obtaining enlightenment is 'right speech'. Not just to say the right thing, i.e. not to lie, but rather to weigh words so as to avoid any kind of annoyance. The Dharma's compassion implies that, what happens to someone else can happen to everybody.

To use words very carefully implies the human right to free speech. A 'spoken word', as a Muslim caliph[10] is once supposed to have said, is one of the three things in life you cannot take back."

"Yes, I guess that's right, although I'm not so sure about there being only three. Anyway, what I always demand of common sense is decency; you have to think very carefully before you speak, otherwise you might easily convey harm."

"You're right. Even poets have in a way to consider their words, although they may have no intention to do harm."

A writer is committed, and the wayfarers agreed about this, to putting his or her images into words; nothing else. But he or she has to be mindful as well. In that regard, they praised the acclaimed late American writer, Ernest Hemingway, for his iceberg theory: the fewer words a writer uses, the more space the reader has in order to find the respective image in him or herself:

If a writer of prose knows enough of what he is writing about he may omit things that he knows and the reader, if the writer is writing truly enough, will have a feeling of those things as strongly as though the writer had stated them.[11]

"Let me ask you: Isn't it the main question why words, language, and speech can hurt, when they just come from a single person and have only to do with that very person?"

"Yes, and that is because nowadays they do not come from the spirit, just from the

---

10 Caliph Umar, c.577 to 644; Three things you cannot take back: a spent arrow, a spoken word, and a lost opportunity
11 Ernest Hemingway in *Death in the Afternoon*

brain alone. The language lacks the 'spirit of brotherhood', lacks the image and manipulates the brain. Think about C. G. Jung, who bases human behavior on the Archetype of the Collective Unconscious. Psychoanalysts like him opened our brains to fathom our hearts as Joseph Campbell, an American scientist and writer stated. He said, Sigmund Freud's bold and truly epoch-making writings of the psychoanalysts are indispensable to the student of mythology; for, whatever may be thought of the detailed and sometimes contradictory interpretations of specific cases and problems. Freud, Jung, and their followers have demonstrated irrefutably that the logic, the heroes, and the deeds of myth survive into modern times. In the absence of an effective general mythology, each of us has his private, unrecognized, rudimentary, yet secretly potent pantheon of dream. The latest incarnation of Oedipus, the continued romance of Beauty and the Beast, stand this afternoon on the corner of Forty-second Street and Fifth Avenue, waiting for the traffic light to change.[12] I understand everything the way, the struggle between ego and self is left in the dark of the unknown. Every human being has to find their own place in the world, has to observe the structure of time and space to consider the relationship to the environment and circumstances."

"Isn't that too much for every human being?"

"No, it's not. Regarding the German philosopher Arthur Schopenhauer: everybody has to live within the place found for them in the world of representation, as he called his concept of the world of our consciousness. Either through active interest or passive consumption, the answer to who we are can be obtained only through feeling or experience. Not helpful are religions concepts that take for granted what mythological description illustrates, or from a knowledge of science that, ignoring the spirit of mythology, claims rationality as its only basis. Although some scientific concepts appear to support, as the Big Bang Theory does, for example, the spiritual concept of Separation. But in general science has failed to replace mythology and provide a world based on the brain alone. Therefor in all the world of representation's turmoil that human beings are living in, some may not find an answer at all and thus remain in the dark of the unknown."

"I don't want to contradict because I won't spoil the afternoon and besides, I know you don't think highly of the mind."

"Oh, why not? … But thanks."

Our wayfarers leave their thoughts and enjoy their way along the mostly empty beach over those thousands and thousands of little Aegean pebbles that so nicely massage the feet while walking. Waves surge softly along the shore, still washing up sea-grass and driftwood after last night's thunderstorm. There is a soft refreshing breeze in the air. Although it is already autumn, the sun almost glows like in summer. From afar, a bizarre little mountain range greets our wayfarers and to the right, across the Aegean, a much bigger one on the Turkish coastline nearby seems to participate in this.

Suddenly, imagine, here on this very beach or elsewhere on other beaches of other islands in the Aegean, imagine a little dark spot on the water. Yet imagination is not truly

---

[12] Campbell, *The Hero with a Thousand Faces,* Prolog

needed. Nowadays it is observable on television and social networks. The world has shrunk. Everything is visible.

The little spot is getting bigger and bigger. People in a boat. A lot. In a tiny boat. On gaining the beach, they begin cheering. Relieved. Others, on different occasions, in other boats, do not cheer. All their strength is spent and some companions may have been lost in the waves as well. But all of them step out of the boats and up in their hopes.

European sun-seeking folks, disposed to enjoying easygoing holidays, face people from Asia and Arabia that arrive exhausted, hungry and desperate on the beaches of the Aegean islands—taking away that holiday feeling.

The more refugees, the fewer the tourists, leaving the locals with a lack of revenue and a surfeit of hardship, leaving them with traumatized children and adults stepping off over-crowded, barely operative dinghies that were already starting to sink the moment they left the Turkish shore. Arriving in the 'promised land' of Europe, most with no more than a plastic bag for their belongings, if anything at all. Stepping off into what they imagine is a future for themselves and where they can receive money to support their families left behind. Coming from areas full of hostility and violence. Overcoming hindrances along their sometimes year-long escape route. Marching hundreds of kilometers through a harsh and alien landscape. Spending all their money only to find the land, they dreamed of, unprepared for them.

What a huge number of peace-seeking people! After arriving, they wait in long lines for registration, for ferry tickets that are only available after registration, should there even be any offered. Or in camps, waiting for asylum, for shelter, food, labor; waiting to get a life. Thousands and thousands of them; and they are not the only ones: others approach Europe by land, and so the overall number must be in the millions.

Thinking of the current situation, the companions agreed that history is filled with escape, forced migration and conflicts in the area the refugees are approaching. These here in the Aegean come in fear and the Europe's citizens are not free from it as well. The aversion that develops among them is apparently mostly based on fear. It comes from the new, the unforeseen, the irrational—in a word: impermanence.
And one of the wayfarers said:

"Impermanence is the ordinary run of things. Here it leads to an obsessive anxiety. A belief that infiltrates that so many cannot be sheltered and fed as required, without supplies running out for themselves. A belief that losing, if all the refugees are let in, their familiar way of life. An anxiety bred of the notion that 'we will all die'. Anxiety, like aversion itself (or its opposite: craving), is brain-driven. For me it is a reflex from the character. Insofar, anxiety is a part of human nature based on that aversion. Although fear or anxiety acts as a kind of a regulative in life, when obsessive, it becomes harmful. Yet if the mind is not driven by obsessive anxiety, there is also this archetypical reflex in human beings that puts people in motion when the situation calls for it. It is called compassion."

"Yes, I guess, you could call it that. As far as I know, it has made itself evident. Nevertheless, the European Union member states have abandoned Greece as thousands and thousands cross the Aegean Sea. All the refugees lining up in the streets, walking in search of the registration camp, hoping for shelter and food overwhelm the authorities. However, there are those islanders and people from abroad who come to help, also some of the tourist do something, even it is the least they can do in that situation."

"You're are right. But, when it comes to the government, it is because the meaning of compassion is in the awareness of people, not institutions. The lack of compassion insofar is a lack of compassion in the people behind the institutions. They are not aware that what happens to someone can happen to anyone. What happened to you can happen to me. The world is permanently on the move, panta rhei.[13] Everyone is connected to everyone else. All the lives and all the suffering. They have not received the message from deep down in the unconscious, the message: when you suffer, I suffer."

On their walk, the companions continued talking about the current situation on the Aegean islands, where, on some days, as many as about five thousand refugees arrive, mainly wet to the skin, thirsty and starving. Most of them have lost all but their stories. Among them, on beaches dotted with swim vests, dinghies and debris, can be seen helpers with water, food, and clothes. Not enough of course, but a godsend for the arrivals. And the helpers give everything they have, bear the loss of revenue from the tourists that have stopped coming and tolerate camps full of desperate refugees in the areas where they live. Those citizens, who do what they think they have to do, are present in all parts of Europe. When helpers are asked why they do it, the answer is, "what else can we do?"

But then, there are those, driven by that obsessive anxiety that burn down refugee hostels, frighten refugees with threats and riots, and blame them moreover for all that has gone wrong: Cold-blooded politicians use that opportunity, take it as a golden one and, try to convince with simplistic arguments that the refugees and globalization are responsible for everything.

"How do you think the poor exiles might feel," one of the wayfarers said, "on hearing these accusations and again having to face what they have tried to flee from: hatred and harm."

"Unfairly treated, I would assume, but blaming others for unfulfilled dreams and wishes even when these are unrealistic or unnecessary is common. Think about Germany in 1933, for example. Then, it used to be 'the Jews and the Treaty of Versailles'."

"You are right, these blamers can't figure what it is that guides the supporters and they hate those politicians that let the refugees in. For those obsessed by anxiety, there is only one consideration, namely denial and the desire to get rid of the refugees, instead of giving shelter, supporting the helpless and comforting the desperate."

"I get it. But on the other hand: I think you are right about all this compassion stuff, but not alone as solution about this issue. I mean—of course, not in a violent way—but the people acting otherwise not entirely being wrong. If you have doubts about whether you can shelter and feed millions of refugees, wouldn't it be careless, even under the impression to avoid migration, not to follow the suggestions of the mind?"

"Of course, it would. The mind is disposed to rational and reasonable action. The

---

13 Heraclitus of Ephesus, Greek philosopher, c 535 to 475 BC

problem is the conflict. First of all, it resides within every human being. Acting from the spirit or from the mind alone is neither spiritual nor reasonable."

"So, we've come back to the niggling problem that people don't understand each other, have we?"

"Yes, take a look at what happened in the countries that the refugees might think of as the 'promised land' when it comes to aversion. There, citizens reminded each other about the growing number of them falling into poverty and having to depend on welfare due to the diminishing rate of employment. Poor and out-of-work people live in problematic neighborhoods. Facing a high drop-out rate from secondary school and children have fewer chances of going to college. Significant numbers of youngsters are without any expectations of finding a job. It's no wonder that reality might be mostly depicted by low welfare and pre-prime-time TV-series."

"And don't forget news-channels. When you watch at intervals hordes of alien-looking people storming the beaches or breaking through boundary fences, those are the images of reality. But that is only what you see. The other reality, the despair and futility inside all of the emigrants, you don't see. It is true, refugees are not invited, they just come—empty-handed, with only the vaguest of plans, and the effect is that they disturb the social life of the host society, but they come after they've been forced to overcome their own fear."

"Right, now do me a favor and consider an image that would depict not just parts of but the entire reality. I won't be so self-opinionated—but you have to find not only the words, but also the meaning; not only the logic in them, but also the spirit."

"You mean, a new hero?"

"Yes."

They continued to walk along in a mood of deep absorption, each harboring an implicit confidence that walking together would always be for the best.

Gino Leineweber, born 1944 in Hamburg, Germany, has been active as a writer since 1998. He has published travel books, biographies, poetry in English as well as in German and was honored with several international awards for his poetry. He also has been the editor of three international poetry anthologies.

https://www.facebook.com/gino.leineweber
http://www.gino-leineweber.de/

Essays, Critiques and Creative Prose

W.A.R. ~ We Are Revolution

Race, the Big Lie
Shareef Abdur-Rasheed

Note: You may not embrace everything in this narrative but the essence is that there is no such thing as "RACE" and that it is important to change the thinking of the mis-educated, mis-informed people of the earth so that it may make a difference to enhance peace and unity with all of the tribes and nations that constitute "Mankind". If that occurs, it will truly be "Revolutionary".

There is NO RACE!! Allah (SWT) in Qur'an Majeed: Surat Al- Hujurat: 49,13 calls his creation male & female humans "Nas" = (Mankind); then, he immediately explains what (Mankind) is comprised of, "Tribes and Nations". Then Allah (SWT) goes on to explain that it is to know one another's 'variety' but that's not nearly as important as all Mankind having "Taqwa" to fear and worship, obey, trust in Allah (SWT) exclusively. That is what determines the rank of one human over another their degree of devotion, Taqwa and only Allah (SWT) can evaluate that. The concept of RACE is evil at its core! It has a subliminal effect that reeks of divisiveness and automatically creates division consciously and subconsciously. Establishing "that other", "them", and us and the "them" is always looked at as less than. It is built into the word itself and, of course, the total concept is a tool of Shaitan. Muslims have bought into this scam as well and refer to "Race, Races", etc. "White institutional racism" has been the scourge of the ages and it is the main agenda that promotes the concept of race. It has been extremely successful in spreading this lie that even people with the highest education have bought into it and become suddenly stupid when it comes to this fraud. It appeals to the arrogance in mankind. Like Shaitan said to Allah (SWT), he wouldn't prostrate before Adam (Aws) because he's made of clay and I'm made from fire. I'm better than him! That's the driving force that allows mankind to accept this monumental LIE! You won't find this Haq (Truth) in the classrooms of the most prestigious universities. This is directly from Allah (SWT) and made clear without doubt.

Remember this? UNITED WE STAND, DIVIDED WE FALL. The false concept of race is probably the most effective tool to divide mankind and create suspicion and blind hatred between the tribes and nations that even often lead to wars and bloodshed. If that is the overwhelming accomplishment that this false concept has achieved historically, then that in and of itself supports the fact that on its face the concept of race, races is EVIL!

Essays, Critiques and Creative Prose

Born and raised in Brooklyn, NYC, Shareef Abdur-Rasheed is a veteran of the Vietnam era, human rights activist and a percussion artist. His spiritual expression comes through the persona of "Zakir Flo" (in Arabic, Zakir means "to remind"). He writes conscious poetry and socio-political commentaries, having authored *Poetic Snacks 4 the Conscious Munchies* and contributed to numerous international anthologies. Shareef is married with 9 children, 44 grandchildren and 4 great grandchildren.

https://www.facebook.com/shareef.abdurrasheed1
https://zakirflo.wordpress.com
http://www..com/shareef-abdur-rasheed.php

$$\mathcal{W}.\mathcal{A}.\mathcal{R}. \sim \textit{We Are Revolution}$$

Racism in America, Maintenance, *and* The Racism Industry
Mutawaf A. Shaheed, AKA C. E. Shy

Racism in America

This opinion piece is for anyone who believes that racism will end in America. The country was set up to profit and survive on separation. A tool to keep people at each other's throats. If racism were to disappear, the country would collapse. There can never be equality, because then those who have been privileged would feel unequal. The past has shown the people in power what would happen if black people were given a chance to prosper. All the black enclaves that did prosper were destroyed by the surrogates of the people in power. Black people did well because they didn't have whites in the way. In every example, when the blacks did well, the NGOs came and destroyed it. It should seem obvious who they were working for by the fact that no apologies were given, no one was held responsible, no restitution was offered for the losses. Blacks were punished for being successful. The reason segregation worked for blacks was that they couldn't do business with whites, even though many wanted to give their money to white businesses. Many felt that white people would like them if they spent their money with them.

One of the ways prisons work is to keep all the inmates at each other's throats. There are many ways that works: making the white criminal feel they are better than the non- whites; positioning these institutions in rural areas where the local racists live; using individuals with low IQs; eliminating contact with people from the urban population; making them believe that the people from those parts of the country are animals and that their duties are to punish those folks. Anything that they do to them is justified like their neighbors, the police. Across the entire spectrum of the country, they are placed in every profession. Their job is to keep blacks in their designated place. The whites who know that this is not the right thing to do will never speak out against it for the fear of some kind of retaliation from their neighbors and friends. They know that things can't change for the better for black people, because they themselves have profited from racism. One example of is the traffic court across the nation. The overwhelming majority, black people, support the court systems as well as many other oppressive institutions. The police forces hunt in black neighborhoods. I'm not suggesting that black people are some kind of angels. That defiantly is not true. Many of their problems are self-inflicted. The lifestyles they lead and the habits they have add to their plight. Things they pursue, they don't need. The lack of self- esteem. Not having a historical context of who they come from. The lack of discipline. Addictions to bad habits. All this makes for a perfect slave to one's passions and subsequently a slave to the system of racism. Any person, black or white, trying to eliminate racism would be considered to have committed an act of treason.
Anyone praying for a racist is a traitor to his people.

Maintenance

When I lived in Sweden some years ago, I became friends with a Swedish guy. He worked as the night manager at the hotel where I lived in. Karl was his name, I think. He was a little older than me, but we hit it off right away. As a manager of the hotel, he knew when all the conventions were coming to Stockholm and the people who had reservations at that hotel. There were conventions like Revlon, Chanel, for which a lot of women were pre-registered. That's how our relationship started. To say things were great would be an understatement. It was the first time I experienced true human-to-human relations with a white person. There was never a hint of racism. I was 19 going on 20 then – being able to detect racism was instinctive.

At some point, he broached that subject. He was amazed that people could be like that, then stated, if he were to come to America there was no way anyone could make a racist remark. At the age I was at the time, I told him, that if he didn't fall in line, he would have to move back to Sweden, because racism was the way of life in the USA. I remember him turning red in the face, shaking his head, saying "no way!" Karl had learned how to speak American English from watching American style movies. Most Swedes spoke English differently, more the Queens English. I met other Swedes just like Karl.

On another occasion, I met and worked with a Polish guy. He migrated from Poland to Sweden with his wife and two kids. I can't remember his name. I do remember him saying that he had never been to America. We worked in a factory that made water clamps. It was a small company and the workers sat relatively close together. After some time, he started asking me about what part of the USA I was from. It was the time in the 60's when the media was displaying the brutality the black people in the south were experiencing at the hands of beasts that were in charge there. He thought that was only in the southern USA, those things happened only in that region and that's because I was from the north where that wasn't the case. I laughed and said that it's everywhere in the USA. He sat there for a few minutes, then began telling me about some of his family members who had migrated to the USA. After arriving in the states, they communicated with him and part of what they told him was that the authorities who talked to them showed them degrading movies about blacks in America; told them to stay away from them; that they were criminals and bums who were dirty; that they didn't want to work, and that they would rape them. Now, you have to keep in mind, he told me what his family told him. It came to me at that moment that he had to be telling me the truth, because as a younger person coming up, I would see the DPs almost running in fear when they saw us anywhere near them. I could never figure out why. What he said woke me up and made me understand what it was. Over the years, I've been told the same stories by other immigrants from various groups – identical stories. One that stands out is that there were some Koreans who were taken on a tour of Harlem as part of their orientation. They were on a bus with windows that had been narrowed, emphasizing the danger they could be in if the black people were to see them.

W.A.R. ~ We Are Revolution

The media has always played its part in maintaining the negative images, along with Hollywood. There are instances where local newspapers have caused cases of lynching and riots. They have underpinned police brutality and the murders of blacks. National news outlets have had to expose the corruption of local politics. The racism is imbedded so deeply that these people feel they have free hand. Any company looking for diversity avoided cities where the racism is displayed with such arrogance and pride. They should continue to do so.

With all this being said, it shows what has been going on consistently forever in this country. That these people have no intention of ever changing because they can't of their accord and that every facility in this country and the people who populate those positions are maintenance workers, whose jobs, sanity and lives depend on being the way they are. They cover everything and position, which effects the way of life. They have never been anything other than the way they are today, nor have their people before them.

It occurred to me that any person who comes to this country has to give up some of their humanity in order for them to fit in. What a human being is or isn't can't be described by sub-humans. Whatever "good people" who may be here are of no effect. The evil ones run the programs. Whatever attempts are made to change the system, they are met with defiance and brutality. Everyone has been affected by the sickness of the society. You can't live in an environment run by people who have no respect or spiritual presence anywhere and not become less than human yourself. Apathy, "Oh well, what the hell" is a part of the sickness. Unfortunately, there is no end in sight. For years now, there have been accelerated rates of suicides, drug overdoses, and wives and husbands killing themselves and their children. Somehow, the message that life has no meaning is being passed along.

Men and women returning from their military service, 15 to 20 a day, are unable to cope with what they were required to do to other humans while in service. All these actions come from the loss of humanity and not being able to handle it. Additionally, having to come to terms that they have been used by the system and then discarded, has had a tremendous negative effect on their psyche. We have people who go with weapons to government offices demanding death for themselves and others, including their own families. The nation remains handicapped by their own rules. Mad men at the helm. Unhappy hours at home, alone.

Why do we have leaderships that are twisted and incompetent? What have we done as a people, as a nation that warrants innocent black men and women being shipped off to prison for things they didn't do, or killed for no reason? One of the more disappointing things about these issues is that these people never learn and they will be worse than ever before. So, get ready for it. It's next to impossible to reach people who have no remorse or conscience, people who are proud of all heinous acts they have done in the name of whatever it is that day, people who think that what they do is in some sick way patriotic.

These same miscreants go to religious services. For what? What are they worshiping? In no scripture can the kind of behavior they exhibit and justify be found. One of the reasons attendances have fallen off with the younger generation at these places is, because they see the hypocrisy and malpractice done by those who try to enjoin the same behavior on them, after they see them going to play like they believe in something other than bigotry and hatred. If younger people decide to do good or evil, they don't need to waste time with a middleman who says, he'll talk to God for them, and they can just go back the strip club. In the meantime, we're stuck with this – with no relief in sight.

The Racism Industry

Racism is an industry, one where the racists work for free. They derive only psychic income and look at it as a bonus. They are like the assembly line workers at an automotive plant. For the most part, they have similar commonalities.

Like any other business, usually the owner is the biggest winner. The racists are in place on every level of society. They have classifications / names, such as "blue collar, middle class, quiet majority, intellectuals, progressive, right-wingers, left-wingers", etc. New names pop up regularly. Different names, the same thing.

It's the iconic lynch mob – called "patriots".

There are those who witness the atrocities and those who physically commit them. All of them come to terms and justify them. This business of racism has made billions for the masterminds and has degraded the workers into being less than human with no conscience or morality. You can never put these things in context as it relates to the past. There is no past, only a continuation of what was initially done. On the surface, racism is there as a success story. For God's sake, keep His name out of it! Some of the more deranged ones try to interject Him to justify their sickness. It always amazes me when they are reminded of their behavior, they get incensed and become enraged. People who are affected by these miscreants call them names, like Nazis, racists, beasts, and so on. The racist is proud of being all those names that people call him / her.

One of the saddest side effects of racism is the Negro and his reaction to the brutality. In his sick state of mind, he encourages them to continue to do what they have been doing to him by forgiving him, even without the permission of the people he has murdered and maimed. Unjustly incarcerated, demeaned, raped and committed every kind of inhumane acts under the sun. All the "good people" stand by and do nothing but shake their heads, go get another drink, then whisper, "What a Shame!" Those "good people" are in positions to do something about the situation, but it's their uncles, brothers, sisters, cousins, fraternity and sorority buddies, etc. who are committing these crimes against black people. Black people are the main targets, because in the minds of the leaders there is the notion, if given an equal opportunity, they would prove to be better at a given task.

There are many examples in their eyes of that being a reality. They look at how a people survived all that has been done to them by them, a people who not only survived but thrived when they were away from them. Remember why blacks were brought here in the first place. It was definitely not to enable them thrive, but to be marginalized, to work for free, to be used and to be dehumanized by the lesser of their kind.
When seeing the people groveling in front of their killers is a testament to their psychological instability and the damage left from the taint of slavery, one must come to terms with the system of racism. It is the lynch pin to a whole way of life that can't be changed. The nation would collapse otherwise. The people who depend on it couldn't survive without it. Equality is not an option. You being equal means for them to be less than equal. There has never been a time in America when there has been fair play for people of color. When a law is passed by the congress to help you, the next congress comes in and changes it back to before. It's called the YOYO effect. You have to ask yourself, if you had a successful business in place, why would you change it – especially, if you are going to put 40 million people in competition with your children and grandchildren? Where is the logic in that? I have white friends. I don't usually refer to them as white; just friends. We know our limits and respect each other by not asking each other to go past our comfort zones. At the end of the day, there are good people and evil people, and that has nothing to do with color.

Racism is a device used to keep people divided, along with other tools like religion, and now, gender. It is important to continue to develop yourselves along the line being educated and having awareness of what you are dealing with realistically. Make sure you check your desires and balance your expectations. Take the middle course in your affairs. There is no such thing as the great individualist. It's a trick to isolate you along with your ego. The people in power work together. Your common ground is being victims. Ask God to forgive you, because you don't have the right to forgive somebody for a person that didn't give you permission to forgive that person on their behalf.

I didn't see the Jews forgiving the Nazis at Nuremburg. They hunted them down then, and still to this day, they are looking for them. In my opinion, any black person who asks for forgiveness of the racist is a sick traitor to his whole race.

Summary and Overview

It becomes difficult to see a clear path to goodness when there are some many distractions and rationalizations for negative behaviors, and when the Status Quo is unwilling to submit to any wrong-doing. The struggle of well-meaning people must continue, just as the maintenance of evil and wrong continues to take hold of the world and various nations.

It has always been assumed by many that all white people think the same and that all black people think the same. Feeding that narrative into the public has been the job of the media and the educational systems to keep us divided / separated. To start with, everyone involved must be honest and take responsibility for their faults and mistakes.

Moving forward, the young people from all sections of the society have to be determined to work for changes; small ones at first. Both parties must identify the trouble makers from their own folks and find a way to deal with them by isolating them from any positive, productive conversations. Boycott or sue any business that favors racism. I refer to any progress made in the direction of equality as the "Yoyo movement". That means, when any progress is made in the wrong direction, as seen by the Status Quo, either the congress or the supreme court pulls the string and takes control of the movement – hence, "Yoyo".

When you deal with folks who are in constant denial, you'll always have these kinds of results. As long as people are willing to sell their values for some worldly gain, any humanity they may have had is lost. Any serious efforts made to alleviate the present conditions can't be done in the public domain.

Finger pointing isn't productive. The first thing one must come to terms with is the fact that the people in control have absolutely no concern for human life, that millions and millions of people have been killed to establish what the people-in-control have. There is no middle course, just right or left or the front or back of the same hand. At some point, there will be an intervention that can't be controlled by anyone. The current pandemic is the tip of the ice berg. I've seen this before, when good people try and stand up for the right thing. It's a waiting game to see who outlasts whom. Unfortunately, the good folks and the "others" have too many things in common in order for a real change to take place on a permanent basis. If people are not willing to change the conditions that exist within themselves, what should we expect?

Mutawaf A. Shaheed, aka "C. E. Shy", has been writing since the seventh grade. He continued writing throughout high school, until he became more involved in sports. After his graduation, he worked at the White Motors Company where he contributed to the company's newspaper with his column, "The Poet's Corner." His regularly featured writings in that capacity constitute his first published work.

https://www.facebook.com/mutawaf.shaheed

Essays, Critiques and Creative Prose

"U", a Single Letter
Kimberly Burnham

In Icelandic, a single letter differentiates between war and peace. "Ófriður" is war, strife, row, dispute, quarrel, rumpus, unrest, and turmoil. The "ð" pronounced like the "th" in *gather*. Take away the "O" at the beginning and "friður" is peace, tame, wise, tranquility, calm and at the root word for *friend* in English. One letter makes the difference between war and peace.

I feel small sometimes in the face of hunger, conflict, hate in the world around me but then I think about Bacha Khan, Wangari Muta Maathai, Carla Peperzak, and so many more who are not well-known, did not have an army behind them or power, and still, they brought peace, safety, and beauty to the world. I often remind myself, "Yes, I am only one person, but one person can do amazing things. One person can profoundly change the world."

There is a math phenomenon where all numbers flow from one, $111111111 \times 111111111 = 12345678987654321$. Everything can flow from a group of ones. When nine ones gather and multiply our talents, anything is possible. One drop of water can join another and another until there is a revolution, a powerful waterfall, a huge ocean that can feed and make a home for many. One artist, singer, dancer can create a masterpiece that enlightens the world with beauty or focuses a generation on a worthy cause, raising awareness, consciousness, and inciting compassion.

We live in a world where a single letter, a single number or a single person can make all the difference. "U", *W. A. R.* or "O" can be the revolution.

Essays, Critiques and Creative Prose

Kimberly Burnham lived in tropical Colombia; in Belgium during the Vietnam War; in Japan, teaching English, and in the diverse international hub, Toronto, Canada. She lives in Spokane, WA with her wife, Elizabeth. She has authored *Awakenings: Peace Dictionary, Language and the Mind, a Daily Brain Health Program* – a book which includes words for "peace" in hundreds of languages.

https://www.nervewhisperer.solutions/
https://www.linkedin.com/in/kimberlyburnham/

W.A.R. ~ *We Are Revolution*

Let Us Be the Change in the World
Elizabeth Esguerra Castillo

We come from one Source, and yet, we witness disparity among individuals. We are One, and yet, what do we see around us? Division, abuse of power, abuse of human rights. It's a cliché to say that everybody wants to change the world but nobody wants to change one's self. But how can there be a true change in the world?

Like peace, change should start within ourselves. Let us all be stalwarts of peace and love among nations. Let misunderstandings end to prevent wars from happening. Let us vote for leaders who are authentic role models and who will bring about betterment in our lives. What makes a good leader, you may ask? A good leader, first and foremost, thinks about the welfare of his / her people. Someone with a heart for people. A person whose heart overflows with love can give more of himself / herself for the sake of others. We need leaders who will be instruments of change in the world and who are full of compassion.

In this time of a pandemic, we should think less of ourselves and think more of others; especially the less fortunate ones. Be the change.

Essays, Critiques and Creative Prose

Elizabeth Esguerra Castillo is a writer and a poet from the Philippines who has received multiple international awards for her work. She is the author of two books, *Seasons of Emotions* and *Inner Reflections of the Muse*. The first one was published in the UK and the latter, in the USA. Castillo contributed to nearly 100 anthologies in the USA, UK, Canada, Romania, India, Africa, Iraq, and Ecuador with her poems.

https://www.facebook.com/lizzyecastillo

$$\mathcal{W}.\mathcal{A}.\mathcal{R}. \sim \textit{We Are Revolution}$$

The Psychology of Racism
The Birth of a Nation: The Rise of the Ku Klux Klan
Kedar Imani

Student: Charles Smith
Instructor: Iris Fortune
Date: August 1, 1998

The most notorious of all secret racist organizations is the Ku Klux Klan, and no other has equaled its strength and power of the 1920s. During its peak, nearly five thousand American white people (people of European descent) belonged to the Invisible Empire. The Klan controlled five legislatures and elected the governors of Indiana, Maine and Colorado between 1921 and 1925. The influence of the Klan was felt from courtrooms to the statehouse and to the floor of the Democratic National Convention. In claiming to protect the values of a white, Protestant America, the Ku Klux Klan eventually began to terrorize, intimidate, slander and murder.

The Ku Klux Klan of the 1920s was the second of three Klan movements; neither the first nor the third of the Klan movements had more than a fraction of enlistments of the second. Klan movements shared the same rituals and traditions, although they were historically different. The history of the Ku Klux Klan found its starting point in Pulaski, Tennessee. Six former confederate veterans, who were missing the thrills and fury of the war, decided to start a night-riding group as a means of "fun". But soon, their "fun" turned into pranks, and then to murders, which were preceded by brutal beatings and the hanging of former Black slaves. With the aid of the hooded Klansmen, who found this particular kind of "fun" to their liking, the Klan soon became the most prominent strains of bigotry ever known to America. General Nathan Bedford Forrest became Grand Wizard in 1869, albeit Pike was among the early leaders who was elected as a means to change the foul air that surrounded the Klan, but to no avail, he was also part of the Freemasonic Order during the 1800s and was very influential.

By 1873, there was hardly any trace of Klan activity. The first Klan existed for less than a decade and had enlisted one hundred thousand members; this served as a model for the far more notorious second Klan. In the early 1870s, 1871-82, the Congress had passed the Enforcement Act, and the Ku Klux Act. These laws made it a felony for two or more persons to conspire or go into disguise with the intent to deprive an individual any civil right or privilege. Many members of the Klan were arrested, but because of the overcrowding of jails, few were ever brought to trial. However, increased Federal pressure dwindled the Klan membership. When President Hayes officially ended reconstruction in

1876, the last vestiges of the Klan disappeared – as a victim of federal investigations, prosecutions, and in some ways, it owns success.

The end of reconstruction signaled the beginning of a new racial cast system in the South – separate and unequal, a system that would remain in place for 100 years. The Klan was very effective in bringing much of that about. Social inequality was the norm, political inequality was the norm, economic inequality was the norm. So, one cannot dismiss the Klan's role as far as moving the South back to its pre-civil war status; certainly, as it relates to race. The number of Blacks murdered in this area will never be accurately known. However, the carnage inflicted by the Klan was staggering. Certainly, hundreds were killed and thousands were injured.

As the 20th century dawned, the Ku Klux Klan was a fading memory; recollections of the hooded order were tainted by popular literature which betrayed the Invisible Empire as a heroic force simply battling to maintain the proper social order. This colorful remembrance would help refuel the Klan's revival. On Thanksgiving Eve 1925, sixteen men gathered atop Stone Mountain, Georgia. As night fell, a towering cross was ignited, and the Ku Klux Klan was reborn. The organizer of the spectacle was a preacher turned salesman named William Joseph Simmons. Simmons was a failed Methodists clergyman who had left the cloth in order to become an internal organizer. Witnesses said that he was as juicy as a rotten tomato and full of emotions and ideas. Simmons had claimed the idea of starting a new Klan came to him in a vision. The birth of the group was simply a matter of timing.

The moment arrived with the release of one of the greatest cinematic achievements of its time. Just days after the Stone Mountain cross burning, *The Birth of a Nation* was released in the South. A film made by D. W. Griffith played to sold-out theaters. The filmmaking was flawless, but the history was not. In *The Birth of a Nation*, the Klan is a heroic force. It is the defender of white womanhood against the ravages of the newly freed slaves – animals, beasts whose main purpose in life was to ravage white women. It's a heroic force; it's a noble force. In the film's climactic scene, a group of the hooded Klansmen rides to the rescue of the film's imperiled heroin as she is threatened by a lust-crazed Black man. Black Americans reacted to the film, *The Birth of a Nation*, with horror, with protest, with demonstrations, as it was an assault on Black America at a time when there were no depictions of Black people as human beings. This film depicted Blacks as beasts while it portrayed the criminals as heroes and saviors. Despite its historic inaccuracies, the film gained legitimacy after President Woodrow Wilson screened the epic in the White House. "It is like writing history with lighting", the President said, "my only regret is that it is also terribly true."

The effect of the film, *The Birth of a Nation* was enormous. It increased hatred towards Blacks, and it made people believe in the history that was portrayed in it. Even unitary ministers endorsed it, and it had a great effect on changing people's attitudes towards Blacks and convincing them that these people really needed to be controlled.

At his Atlanta home, Simmons mapped out the vehicle of control – a handbook called *The Kloran of the Ku Klux Klan* which described the Klan's secret rites and oaths. It defined the meanings of strange names created for Klan ceremonies, regions and officers. Simmons claimed upon himself the title Grand Imperial Wizard, Emperor of the Invisible Empire. As Simmons set forth to build his kingdom, he found recruits hard to come by. But Klan publicists devised a sales' pitch based on the slogan, "100% Americanism".

The new Klan would be a patriotic organization for American-born White Protestants only. It was no longer enough for the Klan to be anti-Black; it now added Jews, Catholic and immigrants to its list of enemies. The recruitment strategies were an enormous success. Within fifteen months, the Klan enrolled more than a hundred thousand new members. The Klan tapped on a fear of millions of Americans. In the twenties, a strong portion of America felt invaded by immigrants. Catholics were growing in numbers, and they felt America was no longer the America they knew. There was a strong feeling they wanted to restore America, and the Klan promised them that too. But as the Klan grew, so did its problems.

Rumors spread about the Klan leadership misappropriating funds. Rank and file Klansmen took to heart the fiery rhetoric used to increase membership; acts of violence began to accrue. The Klan was loathed by bad press in 1921 based on information supplied by a former Klan recruiter. One New York paper ran a horrific Klan exposé which detailed Klan atrocities and financial irregularities. In response, the Congress held hearings into Klan activities. The star witness, the Imperial Wizard Simmons denied all accusations and dazzled the senators. The committee adjourned without taking any action. Amazingly, the investigation had the opposite effect of that which it was intended for. Simmons claimed the publicity was instrumental in aiding the Klan's growth. The moment the newspapers began to attack the Klan, the movement actually grew. Simmons stated, "certain newspapers aided us by using the Congress to investigate us." The result was that the Congress gave the Klan the best advertisement they had ever gotten. He proclaimed, "Congress made us."

Riding a wave of publicity from the newspapers' exposé and congressional hearings, the Klan burst out of the South in an incredible surge of growth. The number of Klansmen rose in every state of the union. New members willingly paid a ten-dollar initiating fee for the privilege of wearing the robe and the hood. Klan recruiters used the church to their full advantage. They persuaded local ministers to join the Klan by offering them free membership and a position of leadership. Klansmen would then make a mysterious call on the congregation. With prior arrangement by the minister, the Klan would meet the congregation and give the minister a donation for his effort in aiding the recruitment for the Klan. When the Klan wrapped its massages in the secrecy symbols of Christianity and the hollowed cloth of the American flag, it found new members who were easily induced to join. In order to recruit, the Klan had to have a powerful massage. If it was, 'join the Klan and we'll lynch a Black or we'll burn a building', very few people would join. For this reason, the Klan would cloak its goals as 'good, Christian, right, moral, just and patriotic'.

By 1922, three million White Americans had joined the hooded order. The stereo type of Klan members as unschooled and savage is inaccurate. The Klan membership in the 1920s represented the cross section of the White Protestant community. Surprisingly, men were not the only ones that hid behind the hoods. At the same time, American women were demanding equal rights. Women who supported the Klan's ideal demanded entrance into the Invisible Empire. Their overture resulted in the formation of The Women of the Ku Klux Klan and other female Klan organizations. At its height, 500,000 women were members of the Ku Klux Klan. With millions now counting themselves as members of the hood order, the Ku Klux Klan became the great social organization for much of White Protestant America in the 1920s.

The Klan demonstrated its popularity with its own form of pedantry and street parades. The marches were exhibitions of might and spectacle. Another custom central to Klan mystery was the naturalization – or initiation – ceremonies when one would be led blindfolded to wide open fields where hundreds would fall to their knees and pledge allegiance to The Invisible Empire. This ceremonial bond, coming together as an association, was to them the means to fascinate people into joining them as in an induction into a fraternity, which gave the inductees the sense of a common purpose. As the Klan membership grew, so did its power. In the national arena, the Klan helped to elect 16 United State senators, five of whom were sworn Klan members. One of the five, Hugo Black, recanted his allegiance when he later became a Supreme Court Justice. From California to New Jersey, voters elected Klan-backed candidates to a variety of state-wide and local offices. Those candidates couldn't run in some places unless they had the Klan's endorsement and support because it had this enormous membership and enjoyed the sympathy of non-members who may not have always condoned the Klan's most brutal acts. Still, the Klan served a role in helping clamp down those dissident elements of society.

The Klan philosophy was one of exclusion. Groups on the out for Blacks, Jews and Catholics were subject to intimidation, economic boycott, and violence. While the majority of members sustained from vigilantism, the Klan was responsible for episodes of racial and religious terror. Most Klan activities transpired in the South, but the Klan's intimidation was felt nationwide. Most violence was directed at Blacks. They were subject to floggings, beatings, and sometimes murders. But the Klan's mission in the 1920s was broader than the intimidation of African Americans. Portland, Oregon's exulted Cyclops once observed

W.A.R. ~ *We Are Revolution*

that the only way to cure Catholics was by killing them. While few Klansmen advocated the murder of Catholics, the anti-sentiment was a lore for new members. Because of their abundant numbers, Catholics bore the brunt of the Klan's religious terrorism. The Klan equally despised those of the Jewish faith. The Jews was a race sat aside; the Klan believed. This ancient blood-rivalry found a real home in the Klan. They developed it, they nurtured it, they spread it. Jews became a natural target for the Klan terror. The Klan was able to operate outside the law because many of the Klan members were the law.

In the last half of 1922, the Moorhouse Perish Louisiana was run by members of the Klan. Because the hooded order had infiltrated law enforcement, Klansmen were confident they could get away with anything, even murder. In the midst of a rabid Klan vigilantism to out spoken critics of the Klan, those against them were murdered, their bodies thrown into a river. Realizing the Klan controlled the town, a desperate governor, John N. Parker, appealed to the Justice Department for help. Due to the activities of the Klan, men were taken out, beaten and whipped. Two men had been brutally murdered. "The conditions of this state are beyond the control of the governor of this state," were the words of the governor as he appealed for help. Numbers of law officers were clearly members of the Ku Klux Klan. After the Justice Department agents discovered the victims' mutilated bodies, the Klan was rescued by the legal system. Two all-white grand juries, each containing known Klan members, heard overwhelming evidence that identified the guilty, yet neither jury brought indictments.

In the mist of the Klan terror, voices of descent were raised. Some states began to fight back with anti-Klan legislations. The most popular law forbade the wearing of masks in public, but these efforts did little to curtail Klan activities. As the Klan weathered external assaults, an internal unrest ignited Imperial Wizard Simmons. The leader of the revolt, a Texan dentist named Hyran Evans sieged command of the Invisible Empire. Although power struggle and scandals sulked its image, in many parts of the country the Klan was just reaching its pentacle of prestige. The greatest success story of the American Klandom was taking shape in Indiana. In the end, it would also be one of the Klan's most despicable stories of horror.

The Klan's dream of complete political power came into origin not in the south, but rather in Indiana. The hood order rose and fell in the Hoosier devised by David Curtis Stevenson. David C. Stevenson was a very talented charlatan and an astute businessman. When the Klan started in a very small way in the southern part of the state, he realized the potential for it. Stevenson championed the purity of womanhood, strongly supported prohibition, and sold the Klan as a political organization. As a result, over 350,000 Indiana residents joined. This large Indiana voting block allowed Stevenson to control Indiana's political apparatus. In the 1924 Indiana election, almost every republican candidate was hand-picked by Stevenson. Stevenson had an interesting strategy: he made candidates sign little pelages that would support him in order to receive the Klan's support. Basically, Stevenson had these elected officials in his pocket with signed papers. Stevenson-backed candidates swept to victory in the November elections. The Klan elected the governor who controlled both houses and the legislature, and the Klan-candidates won a variety of local political offices. Stevenson was at the height of his political power when he, less than a year later, would be confined to a state penitentiary serving a life sentence. In March 1925, Stevenson had ordered his aides to bring a 28-year-old woman, Magg Oerhualcher, to his Indianapolis home. It seems that she was one of the many women Stevenson had a sexual interest in. After forcing her to drink with him, Stevenson whisked Oerhualcher away to a private train car; there he forced her to drink more. Stevenson then proceeded to rape Oerhualcher. He not only raped her but he chewed her like a cannibal; this put her near death. They stopped in a town near Chicago in a small town called Hammond. Oerhualcher was bleeding, crying and scared to death. Oerhualcher ingested tablets of the toxin chemical, myclearic chloride. On the drive home, the spiteful Stevenson refused to obtain medical help for the critically ill woman. "I'll get the law on you", she cried. Stevenson replied, "I am the law in Indiana." Stevenson held Oerhualcher captive in his garage overnight. The following day, his aides drove the woman home, but the lack of medical treatment was costly. When her doctor came, he found she was dying and would not live much longer. In her last days, Magg Oerhualcher destroyed the most powerful man7 in the state of Indiana. Before her death, she had prepared a sworn testimony as to the fact that she was raped and beaten by D. C. Stevenson. Oerhualcher's signature sealed the Klan leader's fate. Seventeen days later, the critically ill women died.

Stevenson was arrested and charged with second-degree murder. He remained arrogant. Surely no jury would convict the leader of the great state of Indiana. But on November 11, 1925, an Indiana jury found Stevenson guilty and sentenced him to life in an Indiana prison. Stevenson was confident that the governor would grant him a pardon, but the Klan leader was shunned by those who owed him favors. Stevenson had a card left to play. Two small black boxes, inside them was the evidence of political misdeeds, bribes, and illegal promises candidates had made to elicit the Klan's support. When no one came to his aid, Stevenson had associates release the contents of the black box. The fallout was dramatic. Governor Ed Jackson was charged with bribery, the mayor of Indianapolis was sent to prison, hundreds of republicans had their careers ruined. The Stevenson affair was a crushing blow to the Klan not only in Indiana, but nationally. The downfall of Stevenson showed the essential hypocrisies and lies of the Klan. They had been championing for the purity of American womanhood, Christianity, championed prohibition, and now there was Stevenson violating all three claims in about the worst way possible.

In an effort to shine a more positive light on the Ku Klux Klan, the Imperial Wizard Evans staged the grandest of all public spectacles. To symbolize the Klan's national power, Evans chose the nation's capital as the location for the thus far largest Klan parade. On August 8, 1925, Evans led 40,000 hooded Klansmen from around the country on a march down Pennsylvania Avenue. It was however the last hurrah for Klansmen in the 1920s. The scandal, negative press, and violence had begun to exact a toll. Disturbed by the extent of the brutality, a mass defection of Klansmen started. Its membership which was over four million in 1925 declined to less than a few hundred thousand by 1928.

It is being opinionated that at that time the Klansmen destroyed themselves. The Great Klan came in as a reformer; however, the Klansmen did not live up to their alleged status. So, in every state the Klan virtually tore itself apart because of its immorality and violence. Its demise in the 1920s, however, did not signal the death of the hooded order. A splintered empire lay under the surface waiting to emerge again.

As the country struggled through the Great Depression, the Klan membership dwindled to about 100,000. The enemy list shifted in the 1930s. Communists and unions replaced Catholics at the top of the hate slate. The center of the Klan activities shifted back to the south. The national Klan organization was dealt a fatal blow in 1944 when the Internal Revenue Services placed a $600,20000, lien against the Klan for back taxes. It appeared as if the Klan would finally be dead. But just two years later, nearly 1000 Klansmen assembled at the bottom of Stone Mountain in Georgia, the home of Klan revivals. The organizer was a 44-year-old Georgia obstetrician, Dr. Sam Greene, which sent out the dramatic 1946-ceremony signal as to how future Klan groups would be organized as self-governing units with no national affiliation. Greene once boosted, the Klan has never been dead, and the Klan is never going to die. His word was perfected.

In the 1950s - 60s, the south became a battle ground over the issues of integration and civil rights. A new breed of Klansmen signed up as soldiers for the fight against Black equality. In May 1954, on a day known as Black Monday to many Klansmen, was the day the Supreme Court outlawed racially segregated public schools. Before then, the Klan's activities had been random and sporadic. They soon would become far more organized and frequent. The Klan was on the losing side of history but wasn't about to go down without a fight. In the 1950s, segregation was the excepted way of southern life. Yet separate but equal was only half-true. Blacks enjoyed very little equality at a time of racial unrest. If you lived in the south in the mid-1950s and you were Black, if you wanted to eat something in a downtown cafeteria, you would have to stand at the end of the counter, take it out on the street and eat it there. If you had to go to the bathroom in the downtown area or in the small towns, you had to wait until you got home. When you boarded the bus, you would have to sit in the back. You lived in a world surrounded by fear, surrounded by not knowing who you were, what you could do, and where you could go. It was virtually a horrific way of living.

Essays, Critiques and Creative Prose

In 1954, the United States Supreme Court struck down school segregation in the historic Brown vs. Board of Education ruling. The decision was met with a finer storm of protest from the south. The Klan aroused again as the walls of segregation began to crumble. There were often asinine remarks like "out here in the woods the beast, don't integrate, out here in the water the fish don't integrate, the fowl of the air don't integrate," or "they still stay segregated, they have more sense than those three or four judges up there". Brown vs. the Board left a terrible impression on the minds of Klansmen and other White people of the south. This meant in their minds that little Black boys could go to school with little White girls. In their minds that wasn't going to happen, not only that they were going to integrate public swimming pools and public facilities, next they'll be integrating motels, hotels and restaurants, and even drinking fountains. So, this gave the Klan a reason to rekindle. Because the national organization was destroyed by the IRS in 1944, there was no longer anything called The Klan. So, independent Klan groups formed all around the south, each separate, each autonomous. The south was a sight of a constant battle of integration. In an attempt to defend the racial cast system, many Klan groups became more militant. Burning a cross along with their secret ceremonies became a Klan-preferred tactic of intimidation. The Klan used other tactics of intimidation, economic boycotts, beatings, and more often, murder. While not responsible for every act, much of the terror experienced then had the letters KKK written all over it.

In the early 1960s, Blacks protested their centuries-long second-class citizenship status in the forms of lunch counter sit-ins, bussed protests, and street demonstrations. Their displeasure became more vocal, more united, and more demanding. The stage was set for a Klan-war against the Civil Rights Movement. In 1960, the longest lasting of all Klan groups was born when an Alabama salesman named Robert Sheldon created the U. K. A. (United Klans of America). Robert Sheldon was a very clever organizer. It is believed that he was extremely dangerous, did not give press interviews, very business-like, very loyal to his ideal – to the point of taking prison terms for refusing to testify before the Congress then give up the Klan's membership list. The U. K. A.'s menacing reputation was cultivated when it played a major role in the savage beating of the freedom riders. Early in 1961, CORE (The Congress of Racial Equality) tested the 1960 Supreme Court mandate of integrated bus stations by sending a group of White and Black riders on a bus pilgrimage through the south. At every station, riders would disembark and attempt to use the segregated waiting room, restaurants, and rest rooms. When the freedom riders arrived at the trailway stations of Birmingham, they were met by a White mob that included 25 members of the U. K. A. The Klan beat those people senseless with iron pipes, chains, and baseball bats. On that day, the Klan beat innocent people and whosoever was there at the time. It was later learned that the Birmingham police had prior knowledge of the attack, but officers had made a deal with the Klan not to intervene. Pressed as to why police didn't intervene, the Police Commissioner Bull Connor explained, "it was Mother's Day; a lot of officers where at home with their mothers."

As the Civil Rights Movement gained momentum, its revered leader became the Klansmen's most despised enemy. There were shouts with demeaning outbursts, such as "the niggers think they have a nigger champion named Martin Luther King; we call him Martin Luther Koon, and if this nigger thinks he can stand up to us, then the White men will stand up to defend what is rightfully his." They hated and despised Dr. Martin Luther King, Jr. because he had carefully planned his Civil Rights Movement which was succeeding despite the Klan's best efforts, which was making their worst nightmare come true. And in the eyes of the Klan, he stood right at the top, directing all of this and pulling the strings. This outraged the Klansmen, making him their "public enemy number one." When Dr. Martin Luther King, Jr. and other civil rights leaders sat foot in Birmingham, Alabama, the Klan was waiting. The bloodiest battleground of the civil rights area was by far Birmingham. In the early 1960s, the town was a racial powder cadge waiting to explode. Birmingham was back then the most segregated city in America, and it had the longest history of aggressive racial violence. Birmingham was once called "Bombingham" by people of the Civil Rights Movement because of the long chain of unsolved bombing of Black homes. The Ku Klux Klan perpetrated much of the violence. As evidenced by the beating of the freedom riders, the city's law enforcement was known for its working relationship with the Klan. This allowed Klan members to believe that they could get away doing just about anything, and they did.

In this charged atmosphere, one the crudest acts of all Klan terror accrued. The 16th street Baptist church was a symbol of the Civil Rights Movement in Birmingham. The secrete chambers served as a staging point for demonstrations against the downtown's segregated public facilities. On the steps of the church, hundreds of Black marchers – most of them children – encountered the extreme force of the Police Commissioner Bull Connor's attack dogs and high-pressure fire hoses. For racial extremists like the Klan, the 16th street Baptist church became a target. On a hazy September morning of 1963, four young black girls attended Sunday school in that church. The day's bible lesson was a love that forgives. The four girls had moved to the basement to take out their choir robes, when suddenly a noise shot through the church like a cannon. A bomb that was planted in the basement ripped through the basement of the house of worship. Once the avalanche of shattered glass, toppled brick and tangled metal were cleared away, a gruesome discovery was made. Cynthia Westly (14), Carol Robertson (14), Addie Mae Collins (14), and Denise Mc Nair (11) were found dead, their bodies laid atop one another.

Comments from Birmingham citizens particularly stressed the following two sentiments: "Of all the bad things that had happened in the south during the civil rights area, to me that was the worst." And, "Four little innocent girls go into church to worship, did nothing to anybody and were viciously killed for no other reason than that they were Black." Within days the police were almost certain the bombers were members of the United Klans of America. The key suspect was none other than "Dynamite Bob Chambliss", the Klansman suspected in many Birmingham bombings. After a very weak investigation, Chambliss and two other Klansmen were convicted only with a minor charge – dynamite possession. That finding was overturned on an appeal. An FBI investigation resulted in no arrest and no other charges.

With the multiplicity of Klan groups spreading throughout the south in the 1960s, one of the most blood-thirsty was known as the White Knights of Mississippi. The White Knights were led by the Imperial Wizard Sam Holloway Bowers. Hard-liner Klansmen of today still revere Bowers. When weighing in the viciousness of the individual, one modern-day Klansman said this of Blowers: "Sam Bowers, three-hundred-and-one to nothing, terrorism, bombs, bricks and bullets, not bullshit, bombs, bricks, and bullets." The same Klansman went on to say that Samuel Holloway Bowers was the greatest Klan leader that ever lived. In 1964, Mississippi was a closed society; only 6% of the state's Black populous was registered to vote. Most Blacks lived in dire poverty and were subjected to intolerable segregated public facilities.

An enclave of northern civil rights groups, called COFO (The Council of Federated Organizations) committed itself to opening up Mississippi. Civil rights organizations decided to target on the theory that if you could break the back of segregation in the south where it was troublesome, you could defiantly disrupt segregation in states where the resistance was not as great. In 1964, COFO brought almost a thousand students to what was called "Freedom Summer" to work on voter's registration and community building. Mississippi acted as if the Mongols was invading it. As the self-appointed defenders of Jim Crow, the White Knights of Mississippi readied themselves for war. The Imperial Wizard Bowers issued an executive directive urging Klansmen to engage in continued violence against the COFO leaders.

The COFO leader the Klan targeted was Mickey Schwerner, a 24-year-old civil rights activist from New York. Schwerner had the attention of White Knights since the day he went to Mississippi to set up COFO offices. In the eyes of the Klan, Schwerner was going against the social mores and was described as a nigger-loving Jew, who would go to cafes and eat at the table with niggers, spend nights as guest in niggers' homes. Worst of all, he was described as an outside nigger-loving agitator. Knowing that the likelihood of violent resistance was high, Schwerner and two other Freedom Summer-workers, the 21-year-old Andrew Goodman and the 21-year-old James Chaney, set out for Mississippi. On June 20, 1964, they inspected the charred remains of the Mount Zion Baptist church near Philadelphia, Mississippi. The church had been torched by the White Knights of Mississippi.

W.A.R. ~ We Are Revolution

After leaving the church, the three civil rights activists were arrested by the Achoo county deputy sheriff Cecil Price on a fabricated charge of speeding. As the three young men sat nervously in their cell, a Klan Hit team assembled. At approximately 10:30 p.m., Schwerner, Goodman and Chaney drove off into the Mississippi night. They would never be seen alive again. Within hours, COFO employees reported the men missing. However, state officials wrote it off as a hoax. When word of the young men reached the White House, President Johnson took strong interest. J. Edgar Hoover was ordered to treat the incident as a kidnapping. The next day, a squad of FBI agents dissented upon the little town of Philadelphia, Mississippi. Just one day after the disappearance of the three civil rights workers, J. Edgar Hoover called L. B. J., with news of the first break in the case. They had found the car. Hoover reported that the car had been burned, and it appeared as if murder was the motive. The discovery of the burned car set in motion an intensive investigation of the incident. Within two weeks of the newsbreak, 153 FBI agents combed through the area, and interviewed locals. Over 400 sailors dragged the swamps in search of the bodies. The FBI began infiltrating the White Knights by enlisting spies and numerous Klansmen as paid informers. This strategy paid off. No more than six weeks after the three men's disappearance, a tip led FBI agents to a farm where their bodies were discovered, buried in an urban dam.

With information supplied from informants and confessions of two Klansmen, the FBI pieced together what had happened. After the three victims left the jail, a Klan death squad and deputy Price followed them on a country road. Forcing their car to stop. The deputy approached them and ordered them into his patrol car. The civil rights workers were then driven to a secluded part of the woods and murdered. The FBI claimed that 18 members of the Klan were responsible for the murders, including Sheriff Lawrence Rainy and Deputy Sheriff Cecil Price. The state of Mississippi refused to bring indictments, but the US Justice Department would take action. The sheriff and the deputy sheriff were involved in the crime; so, this allowed the Justice Department to insert criminal jurisdiction under Federal law. Dusting off the Ku Klux acts of the reconstruction era, the Justice Department sought Federal indictments against the Klansmen, accusing them of depriving the three men of their civil rights. Although Klan groups of the 1960s did not wheel the political power of their predecessors, the political Empire remained active in political matters. Klan members stood active behind elective officials who mirrored their ideals. One prominent elected official greeted a crowd of Klan supporters by stating, "I draw the line in the dust, and toss the garment before the feet of tyranny, and I say segregation now, segregation tomorrow and segregation forever."

In the 1950s and 1960s, political leaders George Wallace and Ross Barnet, of Mississippi, Lester Maddox of Georgia would publicly take a stand against Blacks. It would be rational to conclude that any Klansman would believe that if his leader, his state governor would do this, why shouldn't he?

President John L. Johnson took a public stand against the Klan: "My father fought them many long years ago in Texas, and I have fought them all my life, because I believe they threaten the peace of every community where they exist. I shall continue to fight them because I know their loyalty is not to the United States of America, but instead to a hooded society of bigots." The Klan's hatred of L. B. J. reached its zenith on July 2, 1964, when he signed the Civil Rights Act. Just nine days later, they invoked Johnson's name as they committed a brutal murder. Lemuel Penn was a Black WW II veteran and a high-ranking officer in the Army Reserves. As he and two other soldiers drove down a long stretch of a Georgia highway, Penn was shot and killed by three members of the United Klans of America. One of the Klansmen confessed. When they saw the three Black soldiers on the road, one of them said they must be President Johnson's boys: "I'm going to kill me a nigger." As it so often happened in the previous 100 years, an all-White jury found the Klansmen not guilty.

This is a phenomenon of jury-nullification. The jury hears the evidence which is fairly conclusive, and there is proof, witness testimonies. But because what he did was popular among the all-White jurors, or fit into those jurors' worldview during that troubled period in the south, the perpetrator was set free, let free with the blessing of the jury and the blessing of the society from which the juror and the defendant were commonly drawn. As was the case in Mississippi, the Justice Department appealed to the Supreme Court for permission to prosecute the Klansmen on the basis of Penn's civil rights. The depth into which the FBI infiltrated the Klan was then demonstrated by another tragic killing on a lonely highway.

On March 25, 1965, 12,000 protesters assembled in Montgomery, Alabama. It was the successful conclusion of the Selma-to Montgomery-March for Black voting rights. That evening, Viola Lewhooso, a 39-year-old woman from Detroit and mother of five, shuttled demonstrators back to Selma. Four Klansmen spotted Lewhooso and a Black man traveling together. The Klansmen chased the pair down and shots were fired. Lewhooso was struck in the head and killed. Her passenger survived. Unlike previous FBI investigations of Klan crimes that took weeks or months to solve, the Lewhooso murder was closed with amazing speed. The day after the murder, President Johnson went on national television with an announcement: "Arrests were made just a few minutes ago of four Ku Klux Klan members in Birmingham, Alabama, charging them with the conspiracy to violate the civil rights of the murdered woman. Mrs. Lewhooso went to Alabama to serve the struggles for justice, and she was murdered by the enemies of justice who, as they have done for decades, used the rope and the gun and the tar and feather to terrorize their neighbors."

W.A.R. ~ *We Are Revolution*

Three Klansmen were indicted for her murder and tried. The all-White male jury failed to convict them and they were set free. Later, the three Klansmen were convicted and sentenced to 10 years in prison for violating the civil rights of Viola Lewhooso. Two years after the vicious murder of veteran Penn, two members of the U. K. A. were convicted of violating the soldier's civil rights. In October, 1967, 18 members of the White Knights of Mississippi stood trial for conspiring to deny Mickey Schwerner, Andrew Goodman, and James Chaney their civil rights. The Imperial Wizard Sam Bowers and six other Klansmen were found guilty. Bowers was sentenced to the maximum, 10 years. The White Knights of Mississippi fell into disarray. The combination of FBI probes, congressional inquirers, and Bowers' incarceration fatally crippled the most violent Klan group in the south. The house on American Activities Committee which had investigated the Klan in 1965, released its report in 1967. The report stated what most had already known for a hundred years: "We are forced to the conclusion that the traditional ugly image of the Ku Klux Klan is essentially valid. Preaching love and peace while practicing hate and violence, claiming loyalty to the constitution yet systematically depleting the rights of other citizens. The record seems to be one of moral bankruptcy and staggering hypocrisy."

By the end of 1960, the Ku Klux Klan was a conquered force. The Klan had lost the battle against the civil rights movement. The Klan was brought down in a variety of ways, primarily by the success of the movement. They proved to be ineffective. They murdered people, they intimidated people, but they could not stop the rushing tide of freedom. They could only serve the purpose they told people they were serving. As the decade came to a close, there were scores of crimes attributed to the Klan that remained unsolved. The cruelest among those was the burning of the Birmingham 16th Street Baptist Church. Bill Baxley recalls the day in 1963, when the lives of innocent Black girls were murdered. Bill Baxley later in 1970 was elected Alabama's Attorney General. Within a week of being sworn in, Baxley reopened the case.

After over a seven-year investigation, Baxley zeroed in on the original suspect, the Klansman "Dynamite Bob Chambliss". Baxley's aggressive style won him no friends among the Klan. When the Attorney General received racist letters protesting his continued investigation, Baxley replied on an official state letterhead: "My response to you on your letter on February 19, 1976 is 'Kiss My Ass'." In 1977, Bill Baxley met "Dynamite Bob Chambliss in a court of law, fifteen years after the brutal killing of the four young girls. An Alabama jury found Chambliss guilty of murder. He was sent to prison where he later died.

In 1974, the Klan's national membership was estimated to be only 15 hundred, but new faces would arise from the ashes and lead the Klan to yet another revival. With sanctioned segregation being a relic of the past, the debilitated Klan looked for new issues to battle. In the 1970s, they seized upon the controversy of affirmative action, reverse discrimination, and forced busing. The Klan exploited these issues at public rallies, but was often met with violent opposition. One Black protester took stand and expressed his feelings: "We do not want any trouble; we just want the Klan to go. We will not tolerate this; we will not have it. If we have to die here, well die here. There will not be any Klan, not today, tomorrow never! Death to the Klan!"

The Klan was crippled and in need of guidance. It found a new brand of leader in David Duke. Duke was not a typical Klansman. He rarely wore robes, never dawned a hood. It was seldom that he was caught using racial epithets. The college-educated and good-looking Duke set out to clean up the image of the Klan: "Well, we're not anti-Black so much as we are pro-White. I notice that there's a thousand or so different organizations working for the interest of Blacks or other minorities. We're just an organization that is working for the interest, the ideal and the culture of White people." David Duke is the embodiment of the modern Klan. He is the white collar, buttoned down, well-dressed, impressing Klansman. He really did a great deal to revive the image of the Klan, to make it seem not quite so bad. People would say things like, 'they're not really bad people, look at David Duke, he not so bad, he could be the boy next door.' In fact, he was and is the Klan next door. One might liken this process to the difference between hi-tech slavery (mental) versus chattel slavery (physical). David Duke would be hi-tech slavery.

As Duke worked to build to a political empire, many of his Lieutenants grew critical of their new leader's initiatives. Some deserted the Klan and formed their own more militant groups. Incidences of more Klan-related violence increased. The most shocking incident of Klan-violence took place in Greensboro, North Carolina. On November 3, 1979, members of the Communist Workers Party prepared for an anti-Klan rally. Alliances of the Nazi and Klan party arrived by caravans. Insults escalated into fisticuffs. Moments later, Klansmen inflicted deadly vengeance upon their rivals. Five members of the Communist Workers Party were fatally wounded. A jury decided the shooters acted in self-defense. The murders in Greensboro, North Carolina really shocked the civil rights communities into an awareness that the Klan had not gone away. This event was one of the most shocking and violent incidents connected with the revival of the forth era-Klan.

In the early 1980s, many Klansmen traded in their robes for camouflaged fatigues or the paramilitary uniform. The Texas Klan leader, Louis Beam opened paramilitary training camps. Louis Beam was the bridge between the Klan of the past and the extremist domestic terrorists of the present and future. That would be the Militia, or the so-called Patriot Movement in America. Beam had as many as 3000 armed members in 5 separate training camps in Texas, for a day when there will be a revolution, or a race war. As the Klan gained strength, several organizations fought back. The most influential of the Klan-monitoring groups was started by the Southern Poverty Law Center. After representing a Black victim injured in a 1979 Klan melee in Decatur Alabama, the law center's executive director Morris Dees, created a Klan-Watch. Dees stated that he decided to set up an organization to debunk this whole thing about this "new Klan", and to show it was just the old Klan with new rhetoric that still resorted to violence. The Klan-watch tracked Klan activities, and pursued litigation about the Klan's crimes. The most important case in Dees' fight against the Klan resulted in the demise of the longest lasting Klan group in America.

Robert Shelton's United Klans of America were terror personified in the 1960s, but unlike other Klansmen of that area which succumbed to investigations and prosecutions, the U. K. A. managed to survive. But in March of 1981, the unraveling began. Several members of the Mobile Alabama chapter of the U. K. A. were enraged. After the court case of a Black man who was accused in the murder of a White police officer ended in a miss-trial, Benny Hayes, the tyrant of the U. K. A. Unit 900, was quoted as saying "if a Black may can get away with killing a White man, we ought to be able to get away with killing a Black man." That night, two young Klansmen – the 17-year-old Tiger Knolls and the 26-year-old Henry Hayes, went looking for a Black victim, any Black victim. While cruising the streets of Mobile, Alabama, they found the 19-year-old Michael Donald. The young man was kidnapped and driven to a secluded spot in the woods. They got the rope around his neck, then they put their boots aside his head, pulled on the rope until there was no breath left in Michael Donald. To make sure he was dead, they took a razor knife and slit his throat, put him back into the car, carried him over and hung him in a tree. This was a lynching in its classic sense.

The crime shocked the community. The barbaric murder of this innocent young man was as vicious, as devious, as hideous as any in the long history of the Ku Klux Klan. Based on Tiger Knolls' confession, he and his accomplices had to be convicted of murder. To most, it appeared that the case was closed. Morris Dees felt differently. He encouraged the victims' mother, Beulah Mae Donald to file a civil law case against the United Klans of America. Because the U. K. A. leaders encouraged the violent and murderous act, Dees theorized the Klan organization was also liable. Mrs. Donald agreed to the lawsuit. The 1987-trial lasted but four days. Several Klansmen directed their efforts to commit acts of harassment and intimidation. Tiger Knolls described the murder of Michael Donald, and told how the Klan had encouraged him to commit acts of violence. As he stepped down from the stand, the judge allowed the Klansman to address the court. Knolls turned to Mrs. Donald, spoke her name and began to cry. His lips quivered as he started sobbing. He begged her forgiveness for what he had done to her son Michael. Mrs. Donald just kind of rocked back in her chair. In a very soft voice, almost a whisper, she said, "you know my son. I have already forgiven you." Eye witnesses said that her reaction was probably the most moving moment of the entire trial. The jury returned after just four hours of deliberation and announced a stunning seven million dollars verdict against the United Klans of America. The most durable of all Klan groups had just been destroyed by a southern jury. The Klan had a national headquarters, a thousand square foot building and ten acres of land, and that's about all. That's what Mrs. Donald got. A Black woman ended up with the deed of a probably the most dangerous, violent Klan organization in modern history. The double judgment was a crucial blow to Klans everywhere. Sporadic incidents continued, but for the Klansmen to pursue its terror, there was a lot to lose. They could lose their money, their freedom, even their lives. On June 6, 1997, Henry Hayes was executed for the murder of Michael Donald. He was the first Klansman in modern history to be put to death for the Klan murder of an African American. With a national membership of just over 5000, the Ku Klux Klan today is but a shadow of its former self. Gone are the days when it wheeled great political and social power, gone are the days when it committed vicious acts of terror without fear of repercussions. Today, you can view many groups that are like the Klansmen; they simply are not wearing the white sheets. They take the same stand, they believe in the same principles, they are willing to commit violence. They just don't wear the sheets.

History suggests that the Klan will not disappear. Klansmen have died many deaths only to be reborn whenever many in White America feels threatened. They reawaken as the ideal of intolerance and racial superiority is being taught to succeeding generations. Whether at the peak of its power or barely afloat, the Klan philosophy of hatred and violence had endured since its very beginning. The Ku Klux Klan is America's first society of hate, although diminished, the Klan cannot be ignored. Its collective bigotry lies bubbling under the surface, eager to rise at any moment to battle against racial equality. The former Imperial Wizard Robert Sheldon said the Klan is gone forever. Well, the KKK has been pronounced dead before, but it has come back. Today's diminishing Klan is trying to soften its image, replacing the white robe with the blue suit. The Imperial Wizard now calls himself a National Director. The "N" word is taboo in public. Despite its attempts to moderate, the Klan is generally treated with contempt throughout the south.

In its birthplace, Pulaski, Tennessee, the Klan tried to start an annual march to protest the Dr. Martin Luther King Jr. holiday. Merchants retaliated by closing their shops. Klan members found themselves in a ghost town with no place to eat or go to the restroom. The Klan eventually gave up and called off the march. The plaque on the Pulaski office building where the Klan was formed was turned over by the building owner so the inscription can no longer be read.

Reference:

The Birth of a Nation [Film]. California: Historic Films, 1997
Nelso, Erik (Producers)
Randall David (Director)

W.A.R. ~ We Are Revolution

Kedar A. Imani, 69 years-old, is retired and lives in Baltimore, Maryland. He is a Youth Development Counselor, primary educator, Mental Health Analyst Social Service Coordinator (infants and toddlers), Member of the Sankofa Black Think Tank and Afrikan Diaspora Research, a novice speaker and writer, and an avid reader. His interests include Afrikan History, nature, esoteric-metaphysics, sports and athletics, and research.

https://www.facebook.com/kedar.imani

Essays, Critiques and Creative Prose

W.A.R. ~ We Are Revolution

Your Desire to Defund the Police / Military . . . Is the Revolution! The Revolution Is Happening in Your Mind . . . in Your DNA!
Bill Douglas

Re-examine all you have been told
in school or church or in any book,
Dismiss whatever insults your own soul;
And your very flesh shall be a great poem . . .
~ Walt Whitman

All across America, from Jamal Bowman's crushing of corporate establishment Democrat Elliot Engle . . . to today's (8/7) stunning defeat in Tennessee of corporate democrat Mackler who had 2 million dollars to run on, defeated by Marquita Bradshaw a progressive/left candidate who only had $8,000 campaign donations to Cori Bush taking down a corporate-Democratic Dynasty in Missouri . . . people are tired of corporate/greed candidates, and are choosing those with less money, less slick campaign materials, less TV ads, because they campaign on compassion for their fellow humans. People are choosing candidates who fight for "compassionate solutions."

This is a revolution of consciousness, based on high science that cannot be stopped. Science does not care about what MSNBC, FOX, CNN or the Democratic or Republican power structures think. Science only cares about the truth of reality. Jack White, of the band White Stripes, who campaigned for Bernie Sanders' Campaign said it best in his song, "Denial Twist," . . . "and the truth, there's no stoppin' it!" This revolution you are part of will not be stopped, because the truth of science is on your side.

Tesla's physical science and consciousness research showed him that our well-being and the well-being of all things are inextricably physically intertwined—all of the same energy. Buddha pointed out that an act of harming another absolutely meant that we do not love ourselves, and that the only source of true joy was to be loving to all . . .

"A human being is a part of a whole, called by us a universe, a part limited in time and space. He experiences himself, his thoughts and feelings as something separated from the rest . . . a kind of optical delusion of his consciousness . . . Our task must be to free ourselves from this prison by widening our circle of compassion . . . (*The Gospel of Science: Mind-Blowing New Science on Ancient Wisdom to Heal Our Stress, Lives, and Planet*)."

Essays, Critiques and Creative Prose

It is not these candidates who are making this revolution happen, it is what is, and has been, happening in your own mind, your own consciousness for years or decades . . . and in your DNA since the moment you arrived in this world. Many of us were raised thinking that Dr. Martin Luther King, Jr. carried the entire civil rights movement to victory. To be clear, this is not meant to diminish Dr. King's heroic efforts . . . however, Dr. King, Jr. did not create the power of the civil rights movement . . . it had been bubbling in the soul of the nation, in the consciousness of the people long before Dr. King, Jr. came on the scene. Dr. King, Jr. was "in tune" with the mass consciousness, and thereby was able to surf the wave of this building "collective consciousness for justice", and rode on that fuel to build the mass movement that changed everything.

A tidal wave is happening in government right now! The candidates of today (including the few mentioned above) are being lifted on the wave of your consciousness. They are a product of your yearning for a compassionate society for many years now, and your *yearning* is part of a global homecoming for humanity . . . and you feel it in your DNA even before it happens.

Science reveals that "empathy and compassion" are at the core of your physical being as a human being, and popular media and "popular" society's drift toward the religion of "look out for #1," of "wealth and ruthlessness in business" and society . . . has over these years and decades continually "irritated and insulted your soul (your consciousness)." Science proves this!

Did you know that science has discovered that when a human being enjoys the pleasure of selfish hedonistic pleasures, that it degrades the health of the person's DNA, causing more inflammation, etc.? Yet, science's most important discovery is that when a human enjoys the pleasure of Altruistic actions (actions benefitting others with no personal material reward). It has a healing effect on the person's DNA. DNA is the foundational building block of our physical existence. Science proves that greed and selfishness "insult our very physical structure."

At the same time, science is today also proving that empathetic and compassionate solutions save society big money. In the case of homelessness, for example, studies show that in areas of the U. S. where government began "housing their homeless," those areas saved between $12,000 to $20,000 for each homeless person they took off the streets; saving police, court, jail, administration, emergency room, etc. costs. Compassion saved money.

In the case of healthcare, it would cost $3 trillion to $5 trillion less . . . less . . . less in the first 10 years, to provide Medicare for All to everyone, and the savings would grow larger in time. Compassion saves money!

W.A.R. ~ *We Are Revolution*

In the case of war, our collective souls were insulted when the U. S. A. began the horrific shock and awe bombing campaign on the people of Iraq not long after the turn of the new millennium. It was later learned that the entire rational for this attack, Weapons of Mass Destruction (WMD), was a lie. Millions of Americans were deceived into a war they would not have supported, had it not been for a massive corporate media campaign designed to terrify the public with WMD myths in order to bend their minds to support that war. You see, the human mind is not designed for murdering other human beings.

> "A chief U. S. Army combat historian and author of *Men Against Fire*, S. L. A. Marshall refers to studies by Medical Corps psychiatrists revealing the most common cause of battle failure isn't from fear of being killed, but more commonly from the fear of *killing others* (*The Gospel of Science: Mind-Blowing New Science on Ancient Wisdom to Heal Our Stress, Lives, and Planet*)."

The U. N. Weapons inspectors were working to prove or disprove that WMD were held in Iraq, and the people wanted them to finish their investigation . . . so, the world saw its largest anti-war protest in the history of the planet. All over the world, people came out in the streets to stop the U. S. bombing of Iraq. It was unprecedented in world history . . . but the U. S., the Republicans and the Bush Administration, with the help of corporate military-industrial funded Democrats like Joe Biden and Hillary Clinton, began the shock and awe bombing.

Our DNA shows that "empathy and compassion" are at the core of our physical existence . . . and you may have felt the cells of our body and mind screaming out their insult at that bombing campaign, but what is fascinating is seeing the self-replicating reality that proves this internal "urge" toward empathy and compassion, is reflected in the reality of the larger physical world. We have already seen that in the case of homelessness and healthcare. Compassion is the most economically sound way to solve those social ills, but in the case of war, it is most apparent . . . and perhaps most important.

Negotiation requires empathy, it is the science of logic. If a negotiator cannot feel a sense of what the opponent is feeling, they are by definition an incompetent negotiator. Leading up to the Iraq War, our people had empathy, but our corporate media networks did not, they only had 2% of talking head guests who were opposed or skeptical of war leading up to the bombing of Iraq. 98% of corporate media's talking heads were pro-war according to a Fair Media analysis.

We have spent trillions on the war, and lost trillions in lost productivity and other costs dealing with the damaged souls returning from the wars. More of them have committed suicide upon their return than those killed in actual combat. Polls showed 80% of returning veterans feel the wars were not worth it. So, why do we let our government continue chasing un-scientific cold hard-hearted solutions to society and the world? Well, the election results posted at the top of this article prove that we are not gonna' take this anymore! We are not going to let our government implement policies of cruelty and neglect, because it insults our DNA to do so . . . which is the most profound form of wisdom . . . because our DNA knows that housing homeless, providing healthcare to our neighbors, brothers, sisters, and the people we pass on the street, will save our economy money. And our DNA knows that avoiding war will save our society big money.

Did you know that 61 cents on every (discretionary) tax dollar goes to the military? Dr. King, Jr. said, "A nation that year after year spends more on military than on programs of social uplift, is approaching spiritual death."

My friends, we are no longer dying. These non-corporate compassion-based government officials we are now electing at greater and greater numbers are a sign that our ill nation is beginning to cough out the phlegm of distortion and greed . . . and breathe in the fresh air of compassion.

I will end this article with an excerpt from my new book, which includes the words of Congresswoman Alexandria Ocasio Cortez – the first sign of new life for our nation, when her under-dog campaign took out a 25-year entrenched corporate Democrat in New York City (who had the entire DNC and NY Democratic establishment supporting him), and AOC became the first Justice Democrat to be elected to Congress. If you don't know what a Justice Democrat is, Google it, and get involved, and spread the word.

In conclusion . . . an excerpt from *The Gospel of Science: Mind-Blowing New Science on Ancient Wisdom to Heal Our Stress, Lives, and Planet*:

The Spiritual Consciousness of Government

"At the core, politics at its best is about love. It's about how much we love each other. Really, that's what good politics is. It's about us choosing . . . to love our communities and to love each other, and to treat each other as ourselves . . . and as Dr. Martin Luther King, Jr. said, 'a government budget is a moral document, a budget is a *moral document*' [. . .]"
— Alexandria Ocasio Cortez, U.S. Congress member

"[. . .] in the name of democracy – let us use that power – let us all unite. Let us fight for a new world – a decent world that will give men a chance to work – that will give youth a future and old age a security [. . .]" (Excerpts from Charlie Chaplin's final speech in *The Great Dictator*)

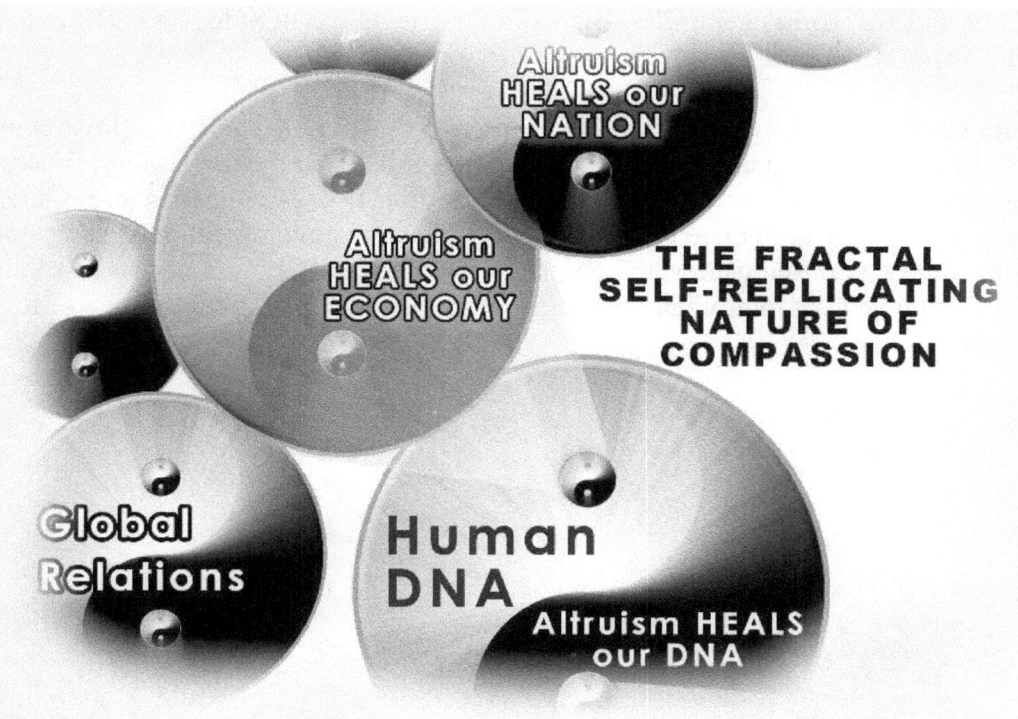

Mahatma Gandhi believed that the only real evaluation of a country's success was found in the state of those most vulnerable in society—and modern politics is beginning to follow his call. In 2013, a *Huffington Post* article by Meredith Melnick, "Denmark Is Considered the Happiest Country," pointed to 3 measurements to determine this: a sense of social support, freedom of life choices, and a cultural ethos of generosity.

Chaos Mathematics' "self-replication" quality carries over, not just to macro-economics, but also to government. As you read earlier, the founder of chaos mathematics' famed article's image of 'a butterfly beating its wings resulting in a tornado thousands of miles away,' goes to the essence of chaos mathematics—that the most subtle initial action at its earliest stage has a massive effect on reality as it unfolds in a series of expanding results. What is the most subtle beginning of everything?

Science shows that the most subtle initiation of everything in the world is consciousness—the beating of the butterflies' wings. How our consciousness beats its butterfly wings determines the unfolding state of our world. You have seen the science showing how altruistic consciousness heals our DNA, the most basic form of our physicality. As love's wings beat in our mind, it lifts our DNA's existence. Meditation unveils this love quality vibrating within us, the DNA heals, and our actions become more loving and compassionate. This unfolds governmental policies, resulting in economic policy which affects us and our world healthfully—and all of this is the result of love's beating its wings within our mind.

This illustrates that Congresswoman Ocasio Cortez's opening quote on 'love being the highest form politics can take,' although it may seem like only poetic oratory, is actually a profound scientific insight. Scientific data of the fractal self-replicating unfolding from consciousness to governmental policies—reveals that any government policy that does not flow from loving consciousness and compassion for the suffering is doomed to failure—poisoned from its very root, within the mind not motivated by our natural state of love and compassion.

W.A.R. ~ *We Are Revolution*

William Douglas is the author of *The Gospel of Science: Mind-Blowing New Science on Ancient Wisdom to Heal Our Stress, Lives, and Planet*. He is the Founder of World Tai Chi Day, whose motto is "One World . . . One Breath," educating the planet on science about how evolving human consciousness will save trillions in future health & social costs.

www.facebook.com/bill.douglas.585
https://smartaichi.com/gospelofscience
www.2012TheAwakening-TheNovel.com/
www.WorldTaiChiDay.org www.WorldQigongDay.org

Essays, Critiques and Creative Prose

W.A.R. ~ *We Are Revolution*

Fragmentation, Mike's Holidays *and* Why Did the Chicken Cross the Road?
Michael Jewell

Fragmentation: The Source of Profanity – Humpty Dumpty's Problem

To profane is to alter our experience of the *nature of being*. The term refers to a manner of perceiving the world: a texture of attitude; a sense of the "other" and simultaneously a sense of "self". Our profanity can affect the world (for example, by leading to the degradation of the environment). But the world cannot *be* profaned. We and world are only profaned *in our eyes*.

The source of profanity is fragmentation. Fragmentation is the result of a descriptive mapmaking process in which boundaries are drawn around parts of the universe-as-whole, thus creating for us objects that exist as distinct entities; compartments experienced as being independent from the whole. This is the essence of objectification. It is a fundamental human activity. Absent the ability to objectify, we would not be human. With it, our access to a stance of reverence is limited.

> "And in all the seriousness of truth, hear this: without 'It' man cannot live. But he who lives with 'It' alone is not a man." – Martin Buber

Objectification is dismemberment and it is through objectification that we create descriptions of the world; maps of content, each confined by our imposed boundaries. In doing so, the world *becomes profaned to us*. Cats don't do it. Weasels don't do it. Beetles don't do it. The term "objectification" does not specifically refer to the *experience* of boundary. Rather, the term refers to the process by which we concretize and stabilize our bounded things through language. This is reification. It is the process through which *our* world is torn to pieces. The resulting Ten Thousand Things are made real to us through the use of nouns and verbs. Cats *experience* boundary, as do spiders and birds. But only humans objectify. Only humans reify.

Profanity does not exist fundamentally. Instead, it is an attitude from within which we experience the world; it is an unfortunate experiential consequence of our unique and highly specialized descriptive and linguistic skill. It is the very expensive price we pay for our analytic competitive advantage over wolves. *Analysis, boundary-making, and mapmaking constitute the Apple of Eden*. However, we did not *choose* to bite. Rather, imbued with our newly serendipitously acquired objectivist mastery, we discovered ourselves peering back across The First Boundary between self and world. And we peered with wonder, terror, and delight.

We Had No Choice

Objectification impedes access to a thoroughly interconnected meeting-with-world. It impedes access to a relational *being-a-part-of "the other"*. When gazing across our imposed boundaries we see the other as object. Simultaneously, we experience ourselves as object.

Other and Self Arise Together
Object beheld by Object

The implications of dismembering the world are, for every human person, vast and concrete. Dismemberment tears to pieces an integrated universe which then becomes misrepresented as a multitude of parts. *This* is the essence of profanity. It jars our deepest sense of meaning. It shatters fundamental value. It limits wisdom. It replaces reverence. It transforms the world into commodity and into a multitude of objects.

The Ten Thousand Distinct Things Suspended in Space

We are repulsed by crass references to sexual body parts because such terms represent the dismembering of organs from the integrated whole, both in being and in purpose. We are offended by ethnic slurs because they bound out entire groups from the whole of humanity thus making them vulnerable to exploitation and abuse (objects are quantified, qualified, valued, or devalued). Objectification dehumanizes persons, signifies land as commodity, and reduces our pets to objects to be owned. In the extreme, slavery becomes the pure embodiment of objectification, an ultimate statement of Life-as-object, Life-as-commodity. But it must be understood that The Problem is not that we fragment the fabric-of-being into a multitude of parts. Rather,

The Problem is that we forget.
We forget that our descriptions of the world – our maps,
our objects-confined-by-boundaries – are competitive conveniences;
mere approximations, mere descriptions.

To fragment, and therefore to profane, is to be human. It is our primary competitive advantage over bacteria. However, this highly refined aptitude does not actually separate us from the thorough fabric of process. *Rather*, it separates us in our own eyes. Humanity is as much a part of The Fabric as are birds, grass, and granite cliffs.

Self / World: The Primary False Dichotomy. The Primary Profanity

W.A.R. ~ *We Are Revolution*

The abyss across which we peer at Eden does not exist except in our experience and in our imagination. Our isolation is self-created, *though we've had no choice*. But occasionally, we and our objects collapse into an integrated whole.

If we are lucky, we then return to our map with a fundamental, persistent, and palpable knowledge of the vast and mysterious whole.

If we are lucky, we then never forget that our maps and descriptions are mere conveniences.

If we are lucky, our existence will then be forever imbued with a deep and pervasive resonant awareness that process – and not object – is the foundation of being.

If we then are lucky, we will forever live immersed in a sense of reverence for all life.

> "When *Thou* is spoken, the speaker has no thing for his object.
> For where there is a thing there is another thing.
> Every *It* is bounded by others; *It* exists only through being bounded
> by others. But when *Thou* is spoken, there is no thing.
> *Thou* has no bounds."
>
> ~ Martin Buber

Mike's Holidays

We *discover ourselves* within the lives we live. Mine has incrementally and relentlessly developed toward profound isolation; an isolation that leads to an overwhelming sadness that threatens my existence.

The threat begins as Thanksgiving approaches and intensifies as people begin asking "*Are you ready for Thanksgiving?*", "*Are you ready for The Holidays?*", "*What are you doing for Thanksgiving?*" The questions emphasize my seeming less-than-ordinary position. It doesn't occur to them that I might have no family and nothing for which to plan. They do not understand how deeply personal these questions are.

Thanksgiving is the worst because it begins a two-and-a-half-month period in which I must, every second day and night, repress the crushing loneliness associated with isolation. It is the worst because it was on Thanksgiving Day that my wife and I had renewed our relationship after 9 years of loss. It was on Thanksgiving Day that I thought that I would finally be where I belonged – with her.

All of the factors assail: the busyness, the smiles, the music, the presents, the Christmas trees, the mind-numbing NPR conversations about recipes, . . . and the requirement at work that I fuel this atmosphere with music. It's an added burden that emails from friends cease about five days before Christmas.

These are the things one notices when immersed in cultural isolation. Everyone is preparing, buying food, wrapping presents, traveling, receiving relatives, cleaning house. They are not writing emails.

I thought I had food in the house yesterday. I thought there was a can of tuna in the cupboard. But no. So, my food during this Christmas day of 2013 consisted of a protein drink, a bit of cheese from a convenience store and a half bottle of white wine.

Many with family would ask: "Why didn't you buy food?", *"It's your own fault that you didn't have food."* (!) But these questions and this challenge, like the others, emerge from ignorance, from a subconscious subjective stance of assuming that the lives of others are like their own and from the belief that we choose our plight. They feel free to take credit and to assign blame. With active empathy they would see that the store is a great threat: large piles of groceries representing intimate dinners and an absence of isolation; friends asking *those questions*; an intensification of loneliness caused by crowds of people who do not see, who do not notice, *and who are preparing*. The grocery store overwhelms with the message: "You are alone". And I with my cart, standing alone in the aisle labeled; "Fewer Than 14 Items".

As The Holidays approach, I pull out the suicide friend, who then resides on my shoulder for two months; mid-November to mid-January when questions finally cease; *"Did you have a nice Christmas?"; "What did you do for Christmas?"; "What did you get for Christmas?"; "How were your Holidays?"; "What did you do for New Years?"; "How was your New Years?"; "Did you stay in town for The Holidays?"* – Me: *"er. . . . I have no relatives. So, during Christmas day each year, I lie in bed attempting to withstand the great weight of The Void, occasionally imaging that she is smiling and happy with her lover and serving her Christmas bouillabaisse. Thanks for asking. Do you have any other questions?"* An occasional person asks me to dinner but sitting amidst someone else's family merely intensifies this sense of isolation. I don't belong at the tables of others' families, not in the familial way that Christmas and Thanksgiving demand.

I have not felt especially close to suicide since the first few years after our divorce. With the TV and lights on all night every night and a bottle of vodka next to my bed, er . . . couch, I was able to mount the heroic effort required to survive. Had it not been for those strategies and for the love of children, I would not have survived. Two years was plenty of time to fully develop *the exit plan*. But now, my intimate and familiar friend resides comfortably on my shoulder during these two months of each year. I take comfort in knowing that He's there.

We have within us a limited volume for containing emotion. When our capacity is exceeded, emotion flows out into the world. The immensity of the pain after she left (the message came by email; *"I want a divorce. I'm sorry."*) was far too great for me to contain. Thus, the agony seemed to pour out of my body, flow in every direction, and then spill over the edge of every horizon. After such an experience, this annual burden of severe loneliness and isolation is not a serious threat. And the presence of my friend on my shoulder – my exit strategy – prevents panic.

Everyone suffers. In context of the overall human experience. the severity of my situation is not extraordinary. But knowing this does not – cannot – help during this annual agony. In every other way, I have been very lucky: I have come to understand the essence of the human experience; my life has been filled with young people whom I love, and who love me. I have had two of the finest friends and mentors imaginable. And at the age of 65, I still have my health. But alas! Relationship trumps everything except for maybe food. So, during these two months, I live amidst a crushing silence, a vacuum, an absence of relationship that can only be understood by those who live it.

Why Did the Chicken Cross the Road?

The chicken discovered herself crossing the road.

The chicken had sensed options but unlike humans, she understood (in her own chicken way) that options are mere imaginations of the future. She had no choice but to cross the road. Thus, she crossed in a state of chicken peace rather than writhing in the confusion and conflict created by an imagination of choice. She crossed with a graceful chicken-confidence born of a surrender of chicken-self. She lacked the desperate need for self-verification and pride that we humans have when crossing the road.

The chicken understood, amidst her chicken wisdom, that the thoroughly woven fabric of external and internal chicken causal factors brought her to this magical road-crossing chicken moment. She therefore embraced her road-crossing destiny without fear, without regret, with great chicken joy, fully committed, and able to face the Vast Chicken Mystery.

"Cluck, cluck, cluck. I guess I'm crossing the road! This feels right!"

Essays, Critiques and Creative Prose

Michael Jewell, who has written extensively in philosophy and politics, is a graduate of the University of Maine. He labels himself a marginalized iconoclastic digging-dog researcher with a relentless reverence for all life. Mike is a technical climbing guide, a professional pianist, and the founder of the Kismet Rock Foundation.

www.facebook.com/michael.jewell.18

W.A.R. ~ *We Are Revolution*

Nachdenken über Frieden
Uwe Friesel

Es gibt ein historisches Foto, anlässlich der Bekanntgabe des Marshall-Plans zum Wiederaufbau Europas nach den Verheerungen des zweiten Weltkriegs aufgenommen, darauf sieht man etliche Herren in dunklen Anzügen nebeneinander auf einer Treppe stehen und applaudieren. In der ersten Reihe stehen der Dichter T. S. Eliot, der Atomwissenschaftler J. Robert Oppenheimer, der US-Außenminister George C. Marshall und der General Omar Bradley. Letzterer trägt Uniform.

Vielleicht wundert es den Leser, wenn ich meine Marginalien zum Frieden just mit den Worten eines (1981 verstorbenen) Generals eröffne. Doch seine beiden Sätze sind heute so aktuell wie damals: "Unsere Welt ist eine Welt atomarer Riesen mit einer in den Kinderschuhen steckenden Ethik", lautet der eine, der andere: "Wir wissen mehr über den Krieg als über den Frieden, mehr über das Töten als über das Leben." Das hat philosophische Dimensionen, wie man sie kaum noch von Politikern erwartet, geschweige denn von Militärs.

Das Foto ist auch deshalb aufschlussreich, weil die vier Männer vier Berufe repräsentieren, die sich sozusagen von Amts wegen mit Fragen des Friedens befassen sollten: ein General, der tatsächlich für sich in Anspruch nehmen durfte, er kämpfe für den Frieden; ein Außenminister, der für seine Aufbauarbeit auch im Land des früheren Feindes zu Recht den Friedensnobelpreis bekam; ein Atomwissenschaftler, der mit seiner Beteiligung bei der Entwicklung der Wasserstoffbombe ins Zentrum des Antagonismus Krieg-Frieden geriet und wegen seiner Skrupel vor einen Untersuchungsausschuss zitiert wurde (der deutsche Dramatiker Heiner Kipphardt machte diesen Konflikt dann mit seinem Stück *In der Sache J. Robert Oppenheimer* zu einem öffentlichen Thema), und schließlich ein gefeierter Dichter und Nobelpreisträger, der aus christlicher Sicht gegen die Weltkatastrophe anschrieb.

Übrigens sind alle vier Amerikaner.

Von Politikern demokratischer Staaten erwartet man, dass sie für den Frieden eintreten. Deshalb war der Angriff auf den Irak mit seinen wechselnden Begründungen auch so schockierend. Doch die wenigsten Politiker sind in ihrem Handeln stets von der Unabdingbarkeit des Friedens motiviert. Nur die Charismatischen unter ihnen finden Worte dafür, die es wert sind, sich ins Gedächtnis der Völker einzuprägen, etwa Indira Gandhi mit dem Satz: "Mit geballter Faust kann man keinen Händedruck austauschen." Oder ihr Namensvater, der Erfinder des gewaltlosen Widerstands, Mahatma (= die große Seele) Gandhi, mit dem Augen öffnenden Halbsatz: "Auge um Auge – bis die ganze Welt blind ist."

Allein diese zwei Sätze stellen weite Bereiche gegenwärtiger Politik als das bloß, was sie sind: armselige Rückgriffe auf Atavismen, bestenfalls auf das nationalistische Vormachtdenken des 19. Jahrhunderts. Schon Willy Brandt bemerkte hierzu: "Nicht der Krieg ist der Vater aller Dinge, sondern der Frieden." Wohl wegen solcher Sätze und entsprechender Taten ist er, neben Gustav Stresemann, der einzige Friedensnobelpreisträger unter deutschen Politikern geblieben.

Um gerecht zu sein: Menschen, die an der Macht sind, haben selten Gelegenheit, deutlich und eindeutig für eine friedliche Politik zu optieren. Meist scheinen die Umstände das Gegenteil zu fordern. Wollen sie trotzdem Frieden stiften, werden sie oft genug von Fanatikern aus den eigenen Reihen umgebracht, wie Gandhi selbst, aber auch der Friedensnobelpreisträger Anwar el Sadat (Ägypten), der schon Ende der siebziger Jahre Frieden mit Israel wollte und dafür von seinen eigenen Offizieren erschossen wurde. Oder umgekehrt der israelische Friedenspreisträger Yitzhak Rabin, den ein ultra-orthodoxer Mitbürger 1995 ermordete, weil er – zusammen mit Jassir Arafat – eine friedliche Lösung in Palästina anstrebte. Jüngstes Beispiel für diesen besonderen Hass auf alle, die friedliche Konfliktlösungen anstreben: die schwedische Außenministerin Anna Lindh. Sie wurde unlängst von einem serbischen Fanatiker erstochen, am helllichten Tage, mitten in Stockholm.

Hass und Frieden sind ein mindestens ebenso relevantes Gegensatzpaar wie *Krieg und Frieden*. Der im Exil lebende XIV. Dalai Lama, ein weiterer Friedensnobelpreisträger, definiert mit Blick auf diesen Antagonismus den Frieden scheinbar ganz privat: "Die Bewahrung des Friedens beginnt damit, dass der einzelne Mensch friedliebend und zufrieden ist."

Es ist schon fast nicht mehr der (buddhistische) Politiker, der aus diesen Worten spricht, sondern, wie im Fall (des Hindu) Gandhi, der Philosoph. Philosophen und Gläubige haben sich häufig aus Überzeugung zum Prinzip des Friedens bekannt und dafür mit Gefängnis, Folter oder gar dem Leben bezahlt. Christus zum Beispiel.

Was indes im zwanzigsten Jahrhundert von den Nazis an Juden und Kommunisten verbrochen wurde, ist so ungeheuerlich, dass kaum jemand, der darüber schreibt, auch nur von fern angemessene Worte dafür findet. Doch mit dem Untergang des Hitler-Regimes hörte es ja nicht auf! Gedenken wir deshalb zu Anfang des dritten Jahrtausends auch der unzähligen Märtyrer einer aufklärerischen *Kirche von unten* in Südamerika und Afrika, am Ende des letzten Jahrhunderts bestialisch umgebracht von der Mordmaschinerie der jeweiligen Diktatoren. Vergessen wir nicht die Drangsalierung bekennender Christen und Juden unter kommunistischer Herrschaft. Das zwanzigste Jahrhundert war das mörderischste seit Menschengedenken. Was um aller Himmel willen kann uns glauben machen, das einundzwanzigste würde humaner?

W.A.R. ~ *We Are Revolution*

Die Idee des Friedens war und ist gefährlich für den, der sie lebt und in Worte fasst. Illusionslos formulierte der brasilianische Bischof Dom Hélder Câmara: "Als Pilger der Gerechtigkeit und des Friedens müssen wir die Wüste erwarten." Der rote Bischof von Rio wurde zwar nicht ermordet, aber wegen seines furchtlosen Widerstands gegen die Folter und des Aufbaus von Basisgemeinden von der eigenen katholischen Amtskirche aus dem Verkehr gezogen. Fast zwanzig Jahre lang hatte er Sprechverbot.

Was erwartet eine Autorin bzw. einen Autor, wenn sie Friedensgedichte schreiben? Jedenfalls kein Idyll. Friedensgedichte sind keine Schäferlyrik. Sie sind auch keine Antikriegs-Poesie, aus jeweiliger Parteinahme möglichst heroisch formuliert. Sie versuchen etwas viel Einfacheres und zugleich viel Schwierigeres, nämlich neue Worte für die ewige Sehnsucht nach Frieden zu finden. Wo ringsum Unfrieden herrscht, halten sie die Momente des Friedens fest. Sie trauern über die Opfer. Sie beklagen das sinnlose Töten. Aus der Position äußerster Machtlosigkeit und Marginalisierung plädieren sie für das Leben.

Die ständige Schwierigkeit besteht darin, der eigenen Angst und grausamen Erinnerung zu begegnen. Vor allem Exilautoren kommen von bestimmten Albträumen kaum los. Und alle, die Gedichte zum Frieden verfassen, müssen sich darüber klar sein, dass ihnen sogar noch der Hohn der eigenen Kollegen sicher ist. "Durchs Höllentor des Heute und Hienieden / Vertrauend träumt er hin zum ewigen Frieden", reimte zum Beispiel Karl Kraus 1918, nach der Erfahrung des Ersten Weltkriegs. Den Millionen von Opfern der Giftgasorgien und Materialschlachten hat er mit seinem kaum aufführbaren Bühnenepos *Die letzten Tage der Menschheit* ein Denkmal gesetzt und war darüber zum Zyniker geworden. Wie auch der große Tucholsky, wenn er 1931 in der *Weltbühne* verbittert feststellt: "Die Gendarmen aller Länder hätten und haben Deserteure niedergeschossen. Sie mordeten also, weil sich einer weigerte, weiterhin zu morden."

Das ist bittere Realität, und wir werden noch erfahren, wie sich die israelische Regierung gegenüber Piloten verhält, die sich weigern, mit ihren Hubschraubern palästinensische Siedlungen anzugreifen. Oder die deutschen, wenn ihre Soldaten in Afghanistan nicht schießen wollen.

Doch macht es sich Karl Kraus allzu leicht bei dem Versuch, mit seinem spöttischen Couplet Immanuel Kants bewunderswerten Aufsatz *Zum ewigen Frieden. Ein philosophischer Entwurf* zu widerlegen. Der Denker Kant träumt nicht, er denkt, zumindest im "Ewigen Frieden". Auch ist ihm Ironie keineswegs fremd. Den Titel zum Beispiel hat er von einem Königsberger Wirtshausschild abgelesen, auf dem der benachbarte Friedhof abgebildet war. Doch genau dieser Gegensatz – zwischen der erzwungenen Friedhofsruhe der Toten und dem fortwährenden Frieden unter den Lebenden – beflügelt sein Denken, 1795, zur Zeit der Französischen Revolution. Fernab im absolutistischen Preußen formuliert er mutig, dass wohl nur Republiken (wir würden heute frei gewählte

Demokratien sagen) in der Lage seien, ein verbindliches Völkerrecht zu schaffen und zu respektieren. Dergleichen galt im Feudalismus als Landesverrat.

Damit denkt Kant seiner Zeit weit voraus. So zwingend ist seine Argumentation, dass der Völkerbund, Vorläufer der Vereinten Nationen, sich bei seiner Gründung ausdrücklich auf ihn berief. In seinem philosophischen Entwurf (vermutlich würden wir ihn heute als Utopie bezeichnen) stehen so bemerkenswerte Sätze wie: "Es soll kein Friedensschluss für einen solchen gelten, der mit dem geheimen Vorbehalt des Stoffs zu einem künftigen Kriege gemacht worden."

Kant kennt sich aus, nach all den landräuberischen Kriegen der Herrscher von Gottes Gnaden ringsum. Scheinfrieden und Rosstäuscherei gelten ihm nicht als reelles Angebot.

Oder: "Stehende Heere (miles perpetuus) sollen mit der Zeit ganz aufhören." Warum? Weil schon die Existenz großer Armeen und Arsenale der anderen Seite den Unterhalt ebensolcher Kriegsmaschinerie nachgerade aufzwingt. Wettrüsten und militärisches Gleichgewicht. Besitzt Pakistan die Atombombe, muss auch Indien sie haben, und umgekehrt. Und selbstverständlich müssen beide Seiten sie erproben, wenn auch nur zu Demonstrationszwecken. *A far cry from Gandhi, indeed*. Doch auch Frankreich muss ja unbedingt ein Südsee-Atoll atomar zertrümmern. Als ob der Ruhm der großen Nation davon abhänge! Und natürlich muss das Schiff der dagegen protestierenden Green Peace-Leute kurzerhand versenkt werden.

Was ist bei Kant oberstes Prinzip des Völkerrechts? "Kein Staat soll sich in die Verfassung und Regierung eines andern Staats gewalttätig einmischen." Sehr brauchbar für die Vereinten Nationen, aber man sieht gleich, warum der derzeitige Präsident der USA (G. W. Bush) und seine Berater die Vereinten Nationen nicht lieben kann, solange sie sich auf Kant berufen. Dabei gehen die Gründung und sogar die Verfassung der Vereinigten Staaten auf ebendieses Denken zurück.

Sieht man nun die Tausende von Büchern und von Friedens- und Konfliktforschungskongressen in aller Welt, die sich auf Kants utopische Schrift von 1795 beziehen, so kann man auch hier feststellen: Kraus hat mit seinem Couplet nicht recht behalten, vor allem nicht mit der Diffamierung, es handle sich um Träumerei. Dagegen steht zum Beispiel die Tatsache, dass der Präsident der einzig übrig gebliebenen Weltmacht mit der schwierigen Aufgabe, das Gleichgewicht der Welt zu wahren, inzwischen ohne die UNO nicht mehr weiter kommt. Auch in Amerika sind ja die kritischen Stimmen, die Kants Sicht der Welt für wichtiger und richtiger halten, nie verstummt. Jüngstes prominentes Beispiel ist ein Buch von Gore Vidal, erschienen 2002, mit dem listigen, Kant abwandelnden Titel *Ewiger Krieg für Ewigen Frieden*. Hier wird auf einen Blick die Absurdität einer Politik erkennbar, die den Teufel mit Beelzebub auszutreiben sucht.

Denn wie ist es meist, auch im Irak? Beide Seiten verschaffen sich Rückendeckung bei der Religion. Saddam, ein ausgepichter Atheist und Mörder, schwadroniert vom Heiligen Krieg, und Bush, ein mit hauchdünner Legalität gewählter Präsident, von seiner christlichen Verantwortung.

Lassen wir doch endlich die Glaubensrhetorik aus dem Spiel! Auch die Kirchen als Institutionen. Das Engagement der letzten Päpste kommt reichlich spät, vor dem Hintergrund einer Geschichte voll blutiger Kreuzzüge, Inquisitionen und sogenannter Christianisierungen. Wahrlich, die Kirche hat ihre Leiden millionenfach zurückgegeben. Wenn sie jetzt zum Frieden aufruft, so beginnt sie gerade erst, sich dem eigenen Anspruch zu stellen.

Verfasser von Friedensgedichten – solche von Rang, meine ich – geben nicht vor, es besser zu wissen. Sie schreiben aus Betroffenheit. Für einige ist persönliche Verfolgung und Vertreibung der Anlass, für andere nur eine Fahrt nach Neuengamme oder eine Reise nach Sarajewo, für dritte ein Medienbericht aus dem Kosovo oder dem Irak, wo immer noch von sogenannten "Kollateralschäden" und "chirurgischen Schlägen" die Rede ist. Für Lyriker zumal gilt es, solche Un-Wörter zurückzuweisen. Sonst fangen wir an, uns an den Krieg als Normalzustand zu gewöhnen.

Reflecting Peace
Uwe Friesel

There is a historical photograph showing the Marshall-Plan's installment after the devastations of the Second World War, on which you can see a group of gentlemen in dark suits standing next to each other and applauding. In the first row there is the poet T. S. Eliot, the nuclear scientist J. Robert Oppenheimer, the US Secretary of State George C. Marshall and General Omar Bradley, the latter wearing uniform.

Maybe the reader wonders why I start my remarks on peace with the words of a general (who died in 1981). But two of his sentences are as actual today as they were then. "Our world is a world of atomic giants with just rudimentary ethics" goes the first, and the second reads "We know more about war than about peace, more about killing than about life." This has philosophical dimensions, as one hardly expects them from politicians, let alone militaries.

Likewise, the photo is tale-telling, because the four men represent professions which should by definition deal with questions of peace: a general who really could claim for himself to have fought for freedom, a Secretary of State who for his reconstructing even enemy territory rightly got the Peace Nobel Price, a nuclear scientist who with his participation in the development of the atomic bomb got into the very center of the antagonism war versus peace and who because of his scruples was cited before an investigation committee (the German playwright Heinar Kipphardt later turned this hearing into a public matter in his drama *In der Sache J. Robert Oppenheimer*). And last not least a celebrated Poet and Nobel Prize Winner, who from a Christian point of view argued against the global catastrophe.

By the way: all four of them are Americans.

Politicians of democratic states are expected to act for peace. Therefore, the attack on Iraq with its everchanging justifications was an enormous choc. But only very few politicians are constantly motivated by the conviction that peace has no alternatives. Only the most charismatic of them find words which will remain in the memory of mankind, for example Indira Gandhi with the sentence "You cannot shake hands with closed fists." Or her namesake Mahatma (= the great soul) Gandhi, inaugurator of nonviolent resistance, with the eye-opening half sentence "An eye for an eye – until the whole world is blind."

These two sentences alone reveal vast stretches of present politics as what they really are: poor regressions on atavism, at best on nationalistic convictions of the 19th century. By contrast, Willy Brandt, former chancellor of postwar Germany, once remarked: "Not war is the father of all things, but peace." Because of such sentences and analogue actions, he remains, next to Gustav Stresemann, the only Nobel-Peace-Prize winner amongst German politicians.

To be fair: people in power seldom have the opportunity to opt clearly and unmistakably for a policy of peace. Mostly, circumstance seems to demand the opposite. If they want despite all obstacles to strive for peace, it often happens that they are murdered by fanatics in their own ranks, like Gandhi himself, but also the Nobel-Peace-Prize Bearer Anwar el Sadat, Egypt, who already by the end of the seventies in the last century wanted peace with Israel and was shot by his own officers. Or, vice versa, the Israeli Peace Prize Winner Yitzhak Rabin, shot by an ultra-orthodox nationalist in 1995, because he – together with Yassa Arafat – was striving for a peaceful solution in Palestine. One more recent example of this special hatred that hits those who strive for peace: the Swedish foreign minister Anna Lindh was stabbed to death by a Serbian fanatic, in plain daylight, in the midst of Stockholm.

Hatred and peace represent as much a dichotomy as war and peace. The XIV. Dalai Lama, living in exile, a Peace Nobel Prize bearer also he, defines in view of this antagonism the notion of peace as a seemingly totally private issue: "Keeping peace starts by every single human being loving peace and being content."

It is rather not the Buddhist politician who talks here but, but – as in the case of the Hindu Gandhi – the philosopher. Philosophers and believers have often adhered to the principle of peace and paid for it by imprisonment, torture or even with their lives. Jesus Christ for example.But then, what has been inflicted by the Nazis on Jews and Communists is so horrible that hardly anybody who tries to write about it can find words. And yet, with the end of Hitler's horror regime the atrocities did not stop! At the start of the third millennium, we must likewise commemorate the numerous martyrs of the "church from below" in South America and Africa who have been bestially done away with by the killing machinery of various dictators. Not to forget the harassments of Christians and Jews under communist rule. The twenties century was the deadliest epoch in the history of mankind. What for heaven's sake makes us believe that the twenty-fist will be more humane?

The quest for peace was and still is dangerous for the one who tries to live accordingly or find words for it. Without any illusion, the Brazilian bishop Dom Hélder Câmara phrased: "As pilgrims of justice and peace, we have to expect desert." The Red Bishop of Rio wasn't decapitated, to be sure. But because of his fearless opposition against torture and for having nourished grassroot communities, he was silenced by his own catholic church. For twenty years, he could not preach any more.

What has an author to face, who wants to write peace poems? By no means an idyll. Peace poems are no pastoral lyrics. They are also not just anti-war poems phrased heroically out of partisanship for one side or the other. They strive for something much simpler and at the same time much more difficult, namely, to find new words for the eternal strive for peace. Where there is nothing but discord all around, they try to capture moments of peace. They mourn the victims. They deplore meaningless murders. From a position of utter weakness and marginalization, they pledge for life.

The constant task is to face one's own fear and ferocious memory. Exile authors, above all, do not succeed do overcome certain nightmares. And all of those who write poems on peace must expect the scorn even of colleagues. "Though inferno and disease // He daydreams of eternal peace" the renowned playwright Karl Kraus rhymes after the butchery of the First World War. In memory of the millions of victims he had written a monumental dramatic epos "The Last Days of Mankind" hardly to be ever performed, and by that work had become a cynic. Much like the great Tucholsky who in 1931 in the periodical "Weltbühne" bitterly deplores: "The military police of all nations would have and indeed have shot down all deserters. In other words, they murdered because somebody refused to keep on murdering."

This is bitter reality. And we shall soon know how the Israel government will deal with pilots who refuse to attack with their helicopters Palestine settlements. Or how German soldiers are dealt with when they refuse to shoot people in Afghanistan.

But to return to Karl Kraus: he makes it all too easy for himself to try to disprove with his ironic couplet the admirable essay "To Eternal Peace" by Immanuel Kant. The philosopher Kant does not dream, he thinks. This holds true especially for "Eternal Peace". He, too, is familiar with irony. The title for his famous essay he has taken from a sign of a pub situated right next to a church yard. But it is exactly this contrast between the eternal peacefulness of death and everlasting peace in life which triggers off his thinking, in 1795, that is, at the time of the French Revolution. Far away from France, in feudalistic Prussia, he has the courage to say that only republics (today we would call them freely elected democracies) will be capable of creating binding international laws and to adhere to them. In feudalism, such reasoning was regarded as treason.

Kant's thinking is far ahead of his time. His arguments are so conclusive, that the League of Nations, forerunner to the United nations, explicitly referred to him when it was inaugurated. In his "philosophical outline" (which nowadays we would call an essay) we find such remarkable sentences as "No peace treaty shall be considered as such when already containing the seeds for future wars."

Kant knows quite well what he is talking about, regarding all the land-grabbing wars of divine right all around him. For his convictions, would-be-peace and deception are no honest offer. Or: "In the future, regular armies shall cease totally." Why that? Because already the very existence of armies and arsenals forces the other side to install them as well. Arms race and military balance. If Pakistan has the nuclear bomb, India must have it too, and vice versa. And of course, both sides have to test them, if only for show. A far cry from Gandhi, indeed. Even civilized France has to devastate a complete atoll in the Pacific Ocean to demonstrate its nuclear power – as if the glory of la grand nation was depending on that! And of course, the green peace ship of the demonstrators against this barbaric act had to be sunk immediately.

According to Kant, what is the highest principle of international law? "No state is allowed to interfere with the constitution and government of another nation." A very useful principle indeed for the United Nations! But one recognizes easily why the present US-President (then G. W. Bush) and his advisors do not love the UN as long as this multinational organization cites Immanuel Kant – not withstanding that both the foundation and the constitution of the US build on his thoughts.

Looking upon the thousands of books written and congresses held meanwhile by peace and conflict scientists all over the world, which are based on Kant's utopian essay of 1795, one can detect also here: defaming Kant's vision of eternal peace as daydreaming as Karl Kraus did has not survived. Even the president of the only remaining world power, the US, when tackling the difficult problem of balancing power meanwhile does not get anywhere without the UN. The number of those Americans who find Kant's historical pledge important has increased. One recent example for this is Gore Vidal's book of 2002 with the witty title "Everlasting War for Everlasting Peace", thus paraphrasing the Prussian philosopher. With one glance everybody can realize the absurdity of casting out the Devil through Beelzebub.

Because, how is it mostly, also in Iraq? Both sides strive to be sanctioned by religion. Saddam, an atheist and murderer, proclaims a Holy War, whereas Bush, a president elected with the thinnest of minorities, blusters about Christian responsibility.

Can't we finally leave out religious rhetoric? Above all from churches and their institutions. The engagement of recent popes comes rather late, if one regards the historical background of bloody crusades, inquisitions and Christianizing campaigns. Verily, the churches have repaid their sufferings by the millions. Crying for peace today just means that they finally try to live up to their own demands.

Writers of peace poems – and here I speak of serious ones – do not pretend to know it all. They write because they are concerned. Some are motivated by personal persecution and expulsion, others by a voyage to a former concentration camp or a trip to Sarajevo. Or they just read about the tragedies of Kosovo or Iraq, which are still talked about in terms of "collateral damage" and "chirurgical blows". For poets it is essential to rebuke such non-words. Otherwise, we start to take war as normal condition of life.

Essays, Critiques and Creative Prose

Photo Credit: Marti Corn, Texas

Uwe Friesel, author, translator (Nabokov and Updike and others). After 1989 first President of the unified German Writers Union (VS). Co-organizer of Writers' Cruises in the Baltic and Aegean Seas, co-founder of the international UNESCO-Centres in Visby and Rhodes. Rewards: Villa Massimo Rome, Writer in residence Hamburg and Berlin. German Literature Fonds.

http://www.uwefriesel.de/art_nouveau.html

Blackbirds
Emerald Stowbridge

Blackbirds have always been interesting animals to me. I sort of felt that they were unique and grand. Much felt they were like a pest or just a plain nuisance. I say they are just misunderstood by those that don't understand them.

Growing up fishing was always a great getaway and adventure for me and a few of my friends. Back in those days, it was common for us to catch the feeling to go fishing. At any time of the day, you could find the three of us somewhere fishing.

Pete, Russel and I decided that we would go fishing. It just so happened that Uncle Lee and Uncle James had the idea to go fishing too. That was right down our alley, mainly because we could ride with them. We wouldn't have to walk in that blistering sun.

Man, we were happy as larks, and to put the icing on the cake, we were heading to a new fishing spot. We wouldn't have been able to walk or ride our bikes there because it was so far away. It was one of Uncle Lee's newly discovered honey holes. Our eyes lit up like a Christmas tree. Pete, Russel and I had never been fishing on this side of town.

We got our gear unpacked and started casting here and there from the bank. It wasn't the best bites, just a few nibbles and tugs that slightly sank the floats. Making our way down the bank, we locked eyes on a boat. And there came the age-old questions from the uncles, "Can ya'll swim?"

"Yes", we replied and piled in with a full head of steam. You couldn't tell us, we weren't about to catch some big ones. All I know is that I caught a few very large golden shiners. They were pretty to the sight, but I heard they were full of bones.

A little water started collecting in the boat, but not enough to frighten us. However, we understood that we needed to make our way back to the bank. Midway there, we could see our uncles waving and yelling; so, we picked up the pace a bit. The closer we got, we could also see some white men coming down the road.

As we approached the bank about 15 yards away, we could hear them. One of them yelled, "Bring the shotgun. I see some blackbirds in the pond." So, me and the crew started looking for the birds too. By the time we reached the shoreline, our uncles hurriedly nudged us along while passing words with the white men.

It became very clear to me, Pete and Russel that those blackbirds were us three. That didn't sit too well with us, and our teenaged tempers flared. Uncle Lee was with that action, but

Uncle James, having a cooler head, insisted that we keep walking backward toward the vehicle. Uncle James later disclosed that the 5 of us were no match for their shotguns or whatever else they had hidden. The entire trip back home was one of watching, making sure that they didn't follow.

I had always heard about the names they called black people, but this was a personal experience that shook me differently. We were kids, and the mere thought of someone willing to shoot us because of the color of our skin . . . this took some time to fathom.

We had a brief discussion about it later on that day, about what happened and possibly why. However, my mind was already set on a path of rebellious thoughts. We talked the incident over for several days and had a lot of folk upset. But as usual, it blew over and things went back to being as normal as it could be.

That was the day when I became a blackbird and learned that some people believe that blackbirds should remain in their own territory. To see a brighter and positive side of this now, I would have to take into account the views and mindset of others and their view of blackbirds. To some, Blackbirds are carriers of intelligence, knowledge and quick wit. These spirited animals are elegant and mysterious. Their black color makes them a symbol of seriousness, mystery, and secrets.

There's a need for a Revolution, because as a child, a young teenager, I should have never faced death because of the color of my skin. The Africans were the architects of civilization that had ruling Kingdoms for thousands of years. They are the reason that we have advanced science and math. They were the creators of so many wonders of the world. A descendant of all that glory and greatness to be reduced to being called a blackbird, raped, murdered and our homeland split between nations that have become dictators from the spoils of pillaging Africa . . . We deserve a Revolution, not because someone else deems it so but because it belongs to us. In closing, I must leave you with the words of one of the great master teachers, Dr. John Henrik Clarke:

"Every single thing that touches your life, religious, socially, and politically, must be an instrument of your liberation, or you must throw it into the ashcan of history."

Emerald Stowbridge is a native of the State of GA; he lived there for 30 years before moving to Texas. He is interesting, with his funny life stories. His wife thinks so at least; she sometimes has to laugh out loud when he tells her certain childhood adventures.

www.facebook.com/emerald.stowbridge

EPILOGUE

About...
Inner Child Press International

In May 2011, the U.S.-based Inner Child Press was founded by William S. Peters, Sr. as a subsidiary of Inner Child Enterprises. The founder already had an extensive experience when his writings and publications are concerned. Mr. Peters' first book went into print without his awareness in 1972. In 2008, he self-published a collection of his own poems, *My Inner Garden*. Inner Child Press grew out of his desire to self-publish his own literary work, which subsequently led to assisting other writers in the publishing process. This journey led to May of 2011.

From its early years on, Mr. Peters' writer-oriented vision and his staff of established writers have been embraced by novice authors as well as those who had been previously published. Inner Child Press has diligently preserved its original mission – writers for writers – as it grew into a globally distinguished publishing company, starting in September, 2011. A poetry contest resulted in the first edition of *World Healing World Peace* (published in April 2012). The call for submission was open to poets from all over the world. This anthology was a significant first step to Inner Child Press entering the paradigm of international recognition.

As time progressed and Inner Child Press began to publish more authors across the globe – individually and in anthologies, its international presence expanded. This growth also led to Mr. Peters and other board members making appearances at international poetry festivals, to include Kosovo, Macedonia, Lebanon, Morocco, Tunisia, Jordan, Palestine, and Canada. They also made multiple appearances across the United States.

Under the tutelage and with the vision of William S. Peters, Sr. and many of the board members, Inner Child Press attained a formidable international image which led to Inner Child Press International. The company had and continues to exude a strong humanitarian and socially conscious stance. Some of the notable anthological works that have been produced are *World Healing World Peace* 2012, 2014, 2016, 2018 and 2020; *Voices from Iraq*; *Kurdish Voices*; *Aleppo*; *Palestine*; *A Gathering of Words for Trayvon Martin*; *Mandela*; *The Balkans*, and *The Year of the Poet* series which features poets from all over the world and is published each month since January 2014. These conscious offerings do not stand alone; for, there are numerous books of consciousness, such as those by Samih Masoud (Jordan – Palestine), Mohammad Iqbal Harb (Lebanon), Hrishikesh Padhye (India), Bassam Abu-Ghazallah (Jordan – Palestine), Fahredin Shehu (Kosovo), Tihomir Jankowski (Macedonia), Mario Rigli (Italy), Laure Charazac (France), Anwer Ghani (Iraq), Bibhas Roy Chowdhury (India), Faleeha Hassan (Iraq), Frank Verkley (Canada), Yasmeen Hamzeh (Jordan), Demetrios Trifiatis (Greece), hülya n. yılmaz [sic] (Turkey – USA), Dr. John R. Strum (Australia), Anwar Nayef Salman (Lebanon), Kolade Olanrewaju Freedom (Nigeria), and Kiriti Sengupta (India), to name a few.

Inner Child Press International is an integral instrument to empower the voices of writers from all regions of the world through literature and strives to leave an essential footnote in the history of humanity and social critique. Ergo, *W. A. R., We Are Revolution*.

Thank you.

Inner Child Press International

'*building bridges of cultural understanding*'

Other

Socially Important

Anthologies

by

Inner Child Press International

Advisory Board
World Healing, World Peace Foundation
human beings for humanity

worldhealingworldpeacefoundation.org

World Healing World Peace 2020

Poets for Humanity

Now Available at
www.innerchildpress.com

the Heart of a Poet

words for a better tomorrow

The Conscious Poets

Now Available

www.innerchildpress.com

Social Distancing

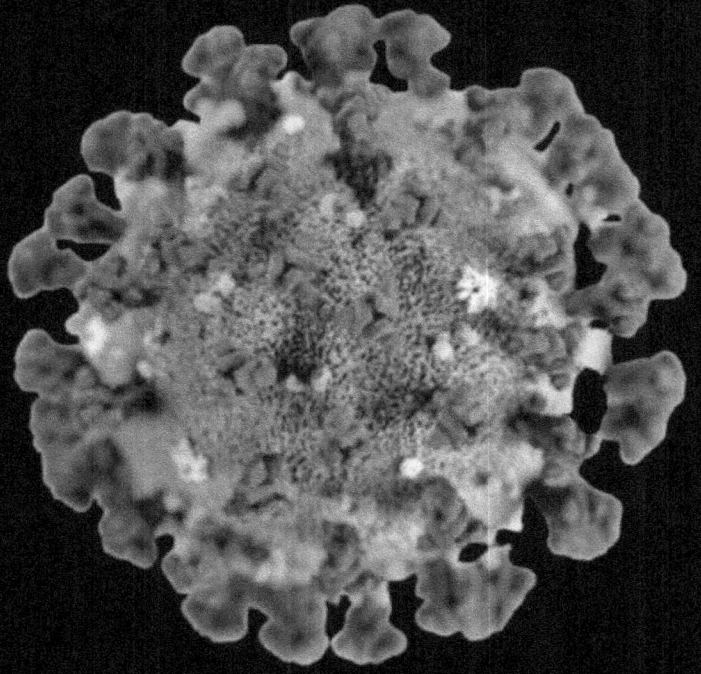

Poets for Humanity

Now Available

www.innerchildpress.com

Now Available at
www.innerchildpress.com

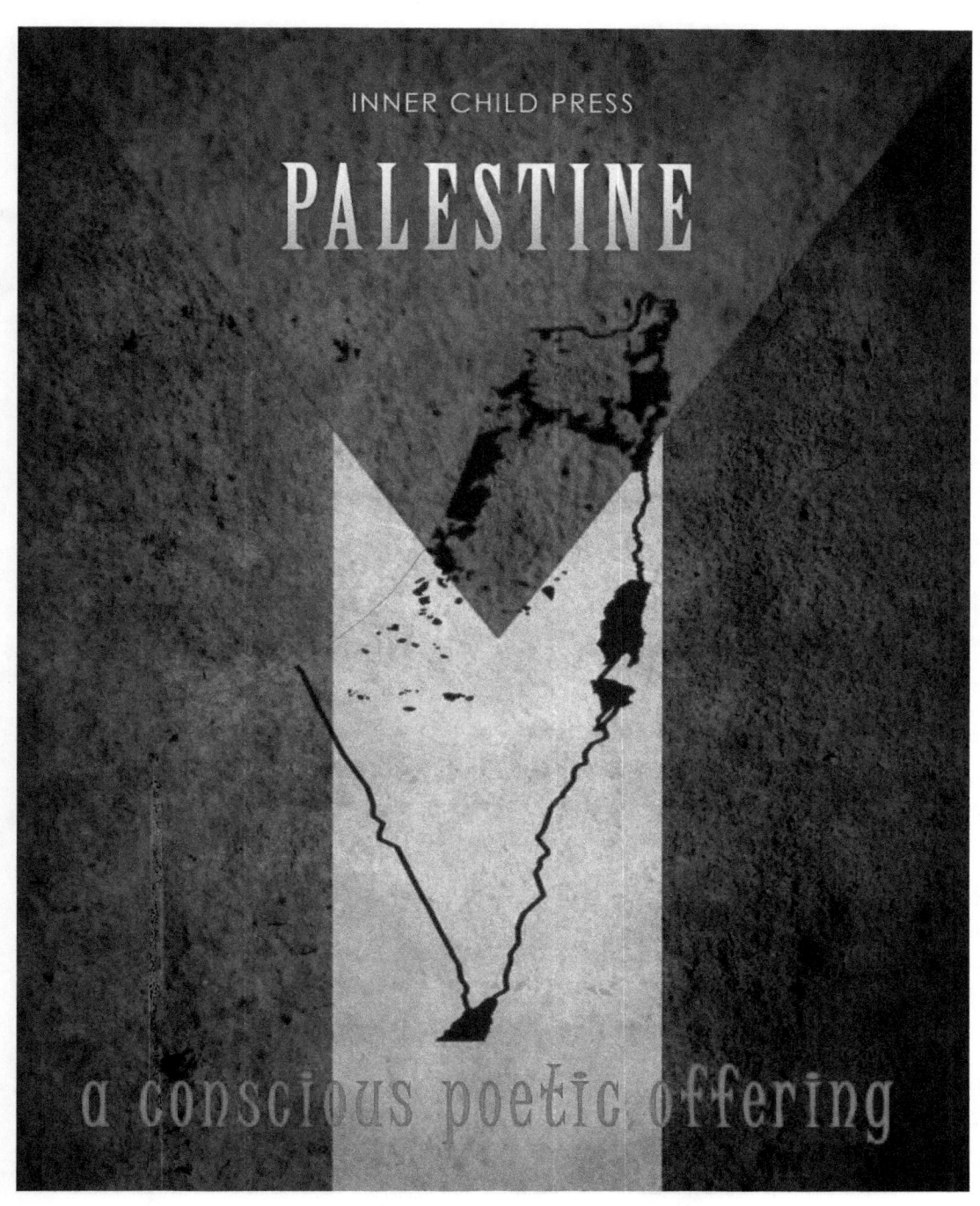

Now Available at

www.innerchildpress.com

Now Available at

www.innerchildpress.com

Now Available at
www.innerchildpress.com

Now Available at

www.innerchildpress.com

Now Available at

www.innerchildpress.com

Now Available at
www.innerchildpress.com

Now Available at
www.innerchildpress.com

Now Available at

www.innerchildpress.com

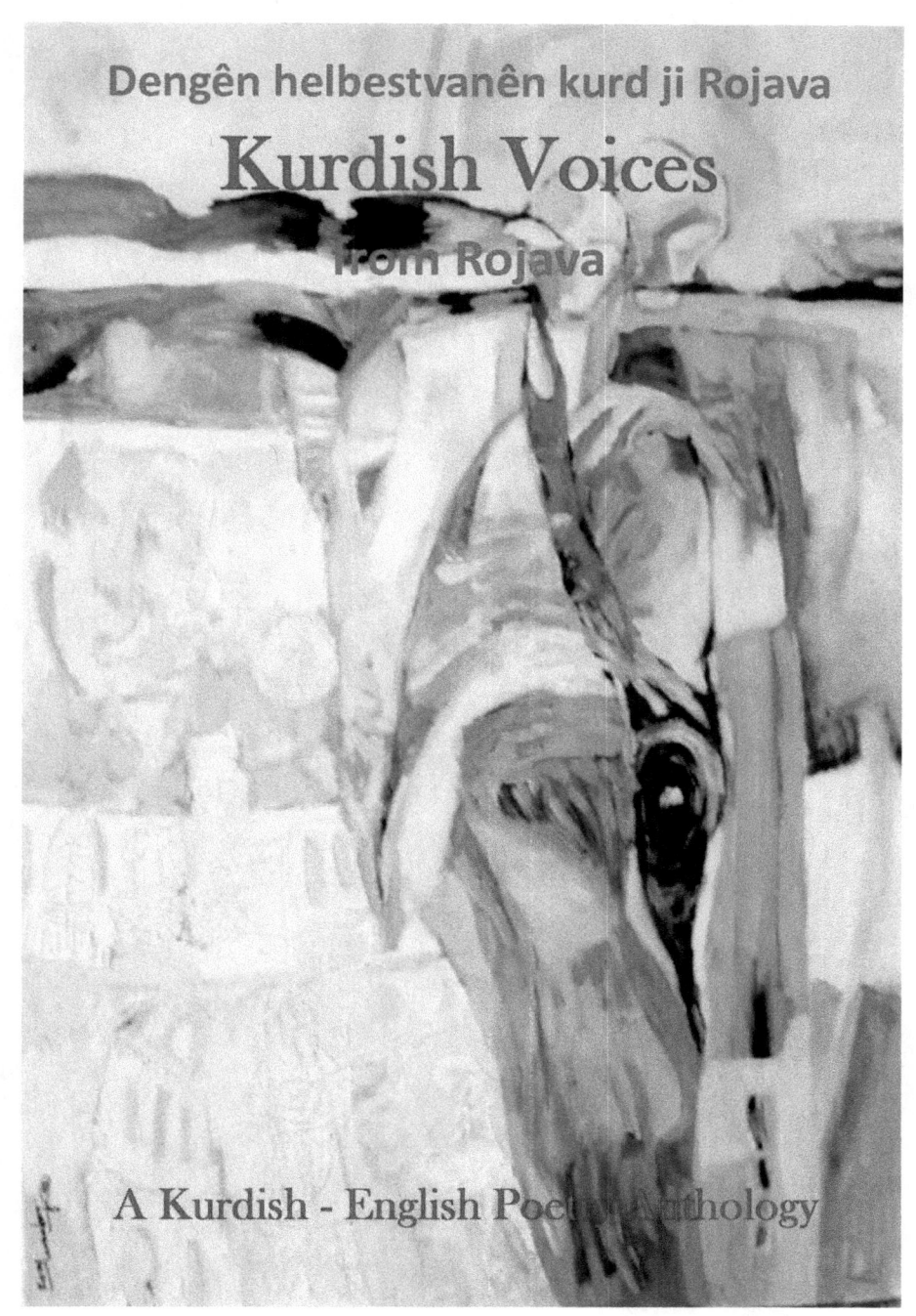

Now Available at
www.innerchildpress.com

Now Available at
www.innerchildpress.com

Mandela

The Man

His Life

Its Meaning

Our Words

Poetry ... Commentary & Stories
The Anthological Writers

Now Available at
www.innerchildpress.com

A GATHERING OF WORDS

POETRY FOR
TRAYVON MARTIN

Now Available at
www.innerchildpress.com

Now Available at

www.innerchildpress.com

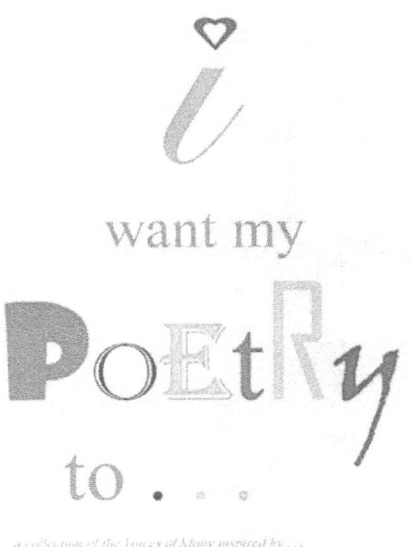

Now Available at
www.innerchildpress.com

Inner Child Press International

Inner Child Press International is a publishing company founded and operated by writers. Our personal publishing experiences provide us an intimate understanding of the sometimes-daunting challenges writers, new and seasoned, may face in the business of publishing and marketing their creative "Written Work".

For more Information:

Inner Child Press International

www.innerchildpress.com
intouch@innerchildpress.com

www.ingramcontent.com/pod-product-compliance
Lightning Source LLC
Chambersburg PA
CBHW081831170426
43199CB00017B/2695